# NINETEEN

## A SALUTE TO STEVE YZERMAN

### JANUARY 2, 2007
### JOE LOUIS ARENA • DETROIT, MICHIGAN

**Executive Editor:** Mike Bayoff     **Managing Editor:** Bill Roose

**Layout & Design:** Norm Klebba     **Editorial:** Bob Duff

**Produced by:** CFW Creative Sports, Inc.

**Printed by:** Tepel Brothers Printing Company

**Photography:** John C. Hartman, Steve Kovich, Dave Reginek, Eric R. Eggly, Mark Hicks, Getty Images, Detroit News, Associated Press, Canadian Press, Windsor Star, Judy Whitney, Lisa Yzerman

**Director of Archives and Historical Documents:** Sharon Arend

January 2, 2007

Dear Red Wings Fans,

We are so pleased to be able to honor Stevie this evening. While we know he has been special to our entire community and Red Wings fans everywhere, he holds a very dear place in our hearts.

Stevie was our first round draft choice at our first NHL draft in 1983, and we have watched that young, fresh-faced, 18 year old boy develop into one of the greatest players and captains in NHL history. We were there when he married his wonderful wife, Lisa, and we watched him grow into a loving father with the birth of his three beautiful daughters. We nicknamed him "Captain Courageous" because he fought back from so many injuries through his determination and grit. He has always quietly displayed the qualities of a true leader.

Tonight Stevie's number 19 will join its rightful place in the Joe Louis Arena rafters along with Sid Abel, Alex Delvecchio, Gordie Howe, Ted Lindsay and Terry Sawchuk. His incredible 22-season career with one team is a remarkable achievement in the world of sports. Only eight other athletes: Alex Delvecchio, Al Kaline, Cap Anson, Stan Mikita, Stan Musial, Mel Ott, Brooks Robinson and Carl Yastrzemski can claim an equal accomplishment.

*Nineteen: A Salute to Steve Yzerman* captures some of the most memorable moments of his illustrious hockey career, and it certainly brings back great memories for us. As citizens of Hockeytown, we hope you will enjoy reliving Stevie's remarkable career as a player, leader and champion in our community.

We congratulate our classy, soft-spoken captain on his numerous accomplishments and milestones on what truly has been a hall of fame career, and we thank him for the pride he has brought to us personally, our team, Red Wings fans and the city of Detroit.

*Mike and Marian Ilitch*
Owners, Detroit Red Wings

January 2, 2007

To all of the loyal Red Wings' fans around North America and the world, a sincere thank you for your support of this great organization during my 22 seasons.

I first experienced what the Red Wings meant to this city during the 1978 Stanley Cup playoffs. I was just 12 years old then when only one game a week was televised, usually from Maple Leaf Gardens or the Montreal Forum. Watching NHL games on Hockey Night in Canada was tradition, and this was the first time that I ever saw a televised game broadcast from Olympia Stadium.

The Wings eventually defeated the Atlanta Flames and advanced to play the Canadiens. The excitement generated from having CBC's broadcast live from Detroit was immeasurable. The atmosphere and intensity displayed by Detroit's exuberant fans, which included the tossing of an octopus or two, was my first encounter with hockey in Detroit and their fans.

As a player, it didn't take me long to generate the same feelings for this organization. Wherever we played, regardless of the city, there was always a strong contingent of Wings' fans supporting our efforts. The best example of this had to be Game 4 of the 1998 Stanley Cup Finals in Washington, where two-thirds of the arena proudly displayed their Red Wings colors. That special night symbolized what it meant to be a Red Wing, for players and fans alike.

I am extremely proud to have played my entire career in the greatest league with and against some of the greatest players in the history of the game. The future of the NHL is bright and I am excited and looking forward to being a part of it as I enter a new phase of my hockey career.

Throughout the course of my playing career there were many who contributed not only to the organization's success, but also to my personal accomplishments. I'm grateful for their efforts and loyalty in making the organization better.

Sincerely,

*Steve Yzerman*

# NINETEEN
## A SALUTE TO STEVE YZERMAN

# Contents

He was playing in the Ontario Hockey League -- the top junior league in the world -- and every NHL team was scouting him so thoroughly. There was nothing not to like about the young center from Cranbrook, British Columbia.

Like everyone else in the scouting fraternity, I knew about Steve Yzerman.

Actually, I first learned of him when I was with the New York Islanders, but he was significantly younger and not draft-eligible at that time.

In 1983, my first year as the Red Wings' general manager, we had the fourth overall pick after the Minnesota North Stars, Hartford Whalers and the Islanders. It was an extremely important draft for the franchise and we had to do our homework thoroughly.

Besides grading a prospect's skill level, the Detroit Red Wings were very meticulous about looking at him from psychological and character standpoint. The proof of that in 1983 was when we got five NHL players out of that draft. That doesn't happen very often, but it happened for us. Our scouts really did their homework.

We had the top kids come to Detroit to spend some time with us, which helped us gauge their character, because we were able to get them out of their homes and get them into an environment that was unfamiliar and strange for them. It helped us try to determine how they would handle themselves when faced with adversity.

I remember us taking Steve over to Tiger Stadium for a baseball game and then we went over to Chuck Muir's Seafood restaurant for dinner. We had a pretty good handle on him from us scouting him, but this time spent allowed him to respond to some questions and for us to see what he was like.

Skill. Talent. Ability. Steve had all of these qualities when we drafted him. And ever since, he's demonstrated nothing short of an impeccable mix of character and heart. He was the cornerstone from which we built the franchise, and he continues to be the face of the organization.

Yet, Steve was the youngest player in training camp that year, and quite frankly, I had talked to him concerning his size and strength. He was only about 155-pounds and not that big and I thought he might not be strong enough to play effectively in the NHL as an 18 year-old. If that was the case, I was going to return him to Peterborough for another year of development.

The good news was that when we started training camp in Port Huron, Michigan, we knew within five minutes that he was the best player on the ice. The bad news was when an 18 year-old player at 155-pounds is your best player we were in real trouble as a team.

I'm often asked to share my favorite Steve Yzerman story or moment. When you think about 22 seasons and over 1,700 games, it's difficult to have just one story.

I fondly remember moments like his first NHL game where he scored a goal and an assist on the road at Winnipeg. The overtime goal that he scored in Game 7 of the second round against St. Louis Blues in 1996 playoffs that lifted the Wings to the Conference finals against the Colorado Avalanche.

I think of Steve coming back from bad knees and being able to play at a high level. I remember the 2002 playoffs, especially the series against the Vancouver Canucks, where he willed us to win after losing the first two games of the series at home, and his will to win even though he was hurting and playing on only one leg. Those are the things that I will remember about Steve. There were hat tricks along the way and the Stanley Cups that we won, and certainly he was just a great, great player.

We in the Red Wings Family are so proud of Steve Yzerman.

Thanks Steve, for far exceeding all of our hopes and expectations.

*Jimmy Devellano*
Senior Vice President
Detroit Red Wings

# NINETEEN

## Career Timeline

### 1983

June 8 - Selected fourth overall by Detroit in NHL Entry Draft

Oct. 5 - Scored first NHL goal against Doug Soetaert and recorded first NHL assist on a goal by Ed Johnstone in his debut at Winnipeg against the Jets in a 6-6 tie

Oct. 26 - Scored first NHL game-winning goal in a 6-5 overtime decision over Buffalo at Joe Louis Arena

Dec. 23 - Recorded first NHL hat-trick against Mike Palmateer in a 9-2 win over Toronto at JLA

### 1984

Jan. 31 - Played in NHL All-Star Game at New Jersey. At 18 years, eight months and 22 days of age is the youngest player ever selected to play in the game

Feb. 17 - Made his first appearance on the cover of *The Hockey News*

Mar. 8 - First NHL fight against Jorgen Pettersson of St. Louis

Apr. 1 - Led Wings in scoring and led all NHL rookies in assists (48) and points (87), setting franchise rookie marks for goals (39), assists and points

Apr. 4 - Made his Stanley Cup debut at St. Louis.

Apr. 6 - Scored first career Stanley Cup goal against Mike Liut of St. Louis

Apr. 8 - Suffered knee injury in final playoff game in a collision with Blues defenseman Rob Ramage

May 29 - Named The Sporting News NHL rookie of the year

June 4 - Named to NHL All-Rookie Team. Runner-up to Tom Barrasso in Calder Trophy voting

Sept. 1-18 - Played for Canada at Canada Cup at the age of 19, winning championship in two-game final sweep of Sweden

Oct. 30 - Registered 100th career point with an assist in a 4-3 loss at Pittsburgh

### 1985

Mar. 2 - Recorded 100th NHL assist on a goal by Darryl Sittler in a 5-2 loss at Minnesota

Mar. 30 - Recorded second NHL hat-trick against Ken Wregget in a 9-3 win at Toronto. Set club record with three goals in one period

Apr. 7 - Finished regular season as Detroit's leader in assists with 59

Apr. 17- May 3 - Played for Canada at the World Championships in Prague, Czechoslovakia, winning a silver medal

Oct. 15 - Signed seven-year contract with Wings

Dec. 28 - Registered 200th NHL point with an assist in a 5-4 win at Quebec

### 1986

Jan. 17 - Registered 100th NHL goal against Clint Malarchuk in a 3-2 win over Quebec at JLA

Jan. 31 - Suffered season-ending fractured collarbone when hit by St. Louis defenseman Lee Norwood, halting his consecutive games streak at 211

Oct. 8 - Named captain of the Red Wings at the age of 21, making him the youngest captain in franchise history

### 1987

Mar. 10 - Registered 300th NHL point with goal against Richard Brodeur in a 7-4 loss at Vancouver

Apr. 5 - Finished as Detroit leader in assists (59) and points (90), the first of seven successive campaigns in succession he would led the club in scoring

Nov. 7 - Recorded 200th NHL assist on a goal by Petr Klima in a 4-3 loss at New York Islanders

Nov. 22 - Awarded first penalty shot of career, but stopped by Boston's Doug Keans in a 1-0 loss at JLA

Nov. 25-Jan. 10 - Garners club-record 22-game point-scoring streak, breaking the 1963 record of 18 games set by Gordie Howe

Dec. 23 - Assessed first misconduct of career in 5-2 loss to Buffalo at JLA

## 1988

**Jan. 3 -** Recorded third career hat-trick against Pokey Reddick in a 4-4 tie at Winnipeg. Tied his own club record with three goals in one period

**Feb. 6 -** Recorded fourth career hat-trick against Brian Hayward in a 5-4 win at Montreal

**Feb. 9 -** Played in NHL All-Star Game at St. Louis

**Feb. 15 -** Registered 400th point of NHL career with an assist in a 6-1 win at Los Angeles

**Feb. 23 -** Beat Philadelphia's Mark Laforest for his 48th goal of the season in an 11-6 loss at JLA to shatter the club single-season goals record by a center set in 1974-75 by Marcel Dionne

**Feb. 27 -** Recorded his first 100-point season with an assist in a 5-4 loss at Quebec

**Mar. 1 -** Became fourth player in Red Wings history to register a 50-goal season, beating Tom Barrasso in a 4-0 shutout of Buffalo at JLA

**Mar. 1 -** Suffered torn posterior cruciate ligament in right knee colliding with a goal post after being taken down by Buffalo defenseman Calle Johansson. Missed last 16 regular-season and first 13 playoff games.

Photo: Courtesy of the Detroit News

**Apr. 2 -** Finished as club leader in goals (50) assists (52) and points (102)

**Oct. 6-16 -** Began season by scoring a goal in each of the first six games, a new franchise record

**Nov. 1-Jan. 4 -** Assembled a 28-game point-scoring streak to shatter the 22-game club mark he'd set one year earlier

**Nov. 4 -** Recorded fifth career hat-trick against Mark LaForest in a 4-3 loss to Philadelphia at JLA

**Nov. 12 -** Recorded sixth career hat-trick against Ron Hextall in a 5-4 win at Philadelphia

**Nov. 18-Dec. 5 -** Recorded club-record nine-game goal-scoring streak, netting 12 goals in this span

**Nov. 25 -** Assessed the first game misconduct of his NHL career in a 6-3 win over Winnipeg at JLA

**Dec. 30 -** Registered 200th NHL goal against Mike Liut in a 4-3 loss at Hartford

## 1989

**Jan. 15-** Registered 500th point of NHL career with an assist in an 8-4 loss at Philadelphia

**Jan. 25 -** Recorded 300th NHL assist on a goal by Joe Kocur in a 6-3 win over Buffalo at JLA

**Feb. 5 -** Reached the 50-goal plateau for the second time in his NHL career, beating Pokey Reddick in a 6-2 win at Winnipeg. Reached 50 goals in 55 games, faster than any player in Wings history

**Feb. 7 -** Played in NHL All-Star Game at Edmonton, scoring his first All-Star Game goal against Boston's Rejean Lemelin

**Feb. 13 -** Scored first NHL penalty shot goal, beating Bob Essensa in a 2-2 tie with Winnipeg at JLA

**Feb. 23 -** Recorded his 56th goal of the season, beating Pittsburgh's Tom Barrasso in 6-6 tie with Pittsburgh at JLA to break the Red Wings single-season goal record of 55 set in 1984-85 by John Ogrodnick

**Feb. 27 -** Recorded his second 100-point season with a goal against Ken Wregget in an 8-1 win over Toronto at JLA

**Mar. 1 -** Became the first Red Wing to register a 60-goal season, beating Mark Fitzpatrick in a 6-5 win over the New York Islanders at JLA

**Mar. 24 -** Became the first Red Wing to register 150 points in a season with an assist on a Lee Norwood goal in a 6-2 victory over Toronto at JLA

**Mar. 29 -** Became the first Red Wing to register 90 assists in a season with a helper on a Brent Fedyk goal in a 4-3 New York Rangers at JLA as Detroit clinched the Norris Division title for the second straight season

**Apr. 2 -** Finished the season with 65-90-155 totals, all single-season Red Wings club marks

**Apr. 6 -** Recorded first Stanley Cup hat-trick against Alain Chevrier in a 5-4 loss to Chicago at JLA

**April 15-May 1 -** Named to all-tournament team at World Championships in Stockholm, Sweden as Canada won silver medal

**May 24 -** Presented Lester B. Pearson Award as the NHL's outstanding performer during 1988-89 season, based on a vote of members of the NHLPA

**June 8 -** Elected as NHL player of the year by The Hockey News, the first Wing to win the award since Norm Ullman in 1964-65

**June 10 -** Married his high-school sweetheart Lisa Brennan in Ottawa

**Dec. 3 -** Registered 600th point of NHL career with an assist in a 4-3 win at Chicago

**Dec. 15 -** Recorded seventh career hat-trick against Jim Waite (1) and Alain Chevrier (2) in an 8-4 win over Chicago at JLA

## 1990

**Jan. 21 -** Played in NHL All-Star Game at Pittsburgh, scoring his second All-Star Game goal against Montreal's Patrick Roy

**Jan. 31 -** Recorded eighth career hat-trick and first career four-goal game against Bill Ranford (3) and empty net (1) in a 7-5 win over Edmonton at JLA

**Feb. 14 -** Recorded ninth career hat-trick against Ron Scott in a 6-5 win over Los Angeles at JLA

**Feb. 18 -** Recorded his third 100-point season with an assist in a 5-5 tie with Montreal at JLA

**Feb. 24 -** Reached the 50-goal plateau for the third straight season, beating Glenn Healy in a 3-3 tie at the New York Islanders. First three-time 50-goal scorer in franchise history

Mar. 25 - Reached the 60-goal plateau for the second straight season, becoming just the sixth NHLer to record back-to-back 60-goal campaigns, beating Greg Millen in a 3-2 loss at Chicago

Mar. 27 - Recorded 400th NHL assist on a goal by Gerard Gallant in a 6-5 loss to Buffalo at JLA

Apr. 1 - Led Detroit in goals (62), assists (65) and points (127)

Apr. 16-May 2 - Led all scorers with 20 points in 10 games, named top forward and to all-tournament team at World Championships in Bern, Switzerland as Canada finished fourth

Oct. 12 - Registered 700th point of NHL career with goal against Hartford's Kay Whitmore in 4-2 win at JLA

Nov. 1 - Registered 300th NHL goal against Peter Ing in a 5-4 win over Toronto at JLA

Nov. 17 - Recorded 10th career hat-trick against Jeff Reese in an 8-4 win at Toronto, scoring a natural hat-trick on three successive shots. Tied club records with three goals in one period and four points in one period

Dec. 22 - Recorded 11th career hat-trick against Stephane Beauregard (2) and Bob Essensa (1) in a 5-2 win at Winnipeg

## 1991

Jan. 19 - Played in NHL All-Star Game at Chicago

Jan. 26 - Recorded 2nd career hat-trick against Vince Riendeau in a 5-4 loss at St. Louis

Mar. 10 - Recorded his fourth 100-point season with a goal against Pat Jablonski in a 4-1 win at St. Louis

Mar. 30 - Reached the 50-goal plateau for the fourth straight season, beating Mike Richter in a 6-5 win over the New York Rangers at JLA

Mar. 31 - Registered 800th point of NHL career with a goal against Ed Belfour in a 5-1 loss at Chicago

Mar. 31 - Led Detroit in goals (51), assists (57) and points (108)

Apr. 4 - Recorded second Stanley Cup hat-trick against Vincent Riendeau (2) and Pat Jablonski (1) in a 6-3 win at St. Louis

Dec. 12 - Recorded 13th career hat-trick against Mike Vernon in a 5-2 win over Calgary at JLA

## 1992

Jan. 3 - Scored second career penalty shot goal against Grant Fuhr in 6-4 win over Toronto at JLA

Jan. 18 - Played in NHL All-Star Game at Philadelphia

Jan. 29 - Recorded 14th career hat-trick against Daren Puppa in a 4-4 tie with Buffalo at JLA

Jan. 29 - Scored third career penalty shot goal against Daren Puppa in a 4-4 tie with Buffalo at JLA

Jan. 29-Feb. 12 - Tied club record nine-game goal-scoring streak, netting 14 goals during this span

Feb. 11 - Recorded 500th NHL assist on a goal by Keith Primeau in a 4-3 loss at Toronto

Apr. 14 - Registered 900th point of NHL career with a goal against Darcy Wakaluk in a 7-4 win at Minnesota

Apr. 14 - Recorded his fifth 100-point season with a goal against Darcy Wakaluk in a 7-4 win at Minnesota

Apr. 14 - Recorded 15th career hat-trick against Darcy Wakaluk in a 7-4 win at Minnesota

Apr. 14 - Tied Shawn Burr's club record with two shorthanded goals in a 7-4 win at Minnesota

Apr. 14 - Led Detroit in goals (45), assists (58) and points (103)

Oct. 13 - Recorded 600th NHL assist on a goal by Sergei Fedorov in a 5-2 win over St. Louis at JLA

Oct. 24 - Recorded 16th career hat-trick against Curtis Joseph (1) and Guy Hebert (2) in a 6-1 win at St. Louis

Nov. 13 - Registered 400th NHL goal against Tom Barrasso in an 8-0 win over Pittsburgh at JLA

## 1993

Jan. 26 - Recorded 17th career hat-trick against Mike Vernon in a 9-1 win at Calgary

Feb. 6 - Played in NHL All-Star Game at Montreal

Feb. 14 - Recorded 18th career hat-trick against Ed Belfour in a 5-3 win at Chicago

Feb. 24 - Registered 1,000th point of NHL career with an assist in a 10-7 loss at Buffalo. Third Wing to collect 1,000 points (Gordie Howe, Alex Delvecchio)

Feb. 24 - Recorded his sixth 100-point season with an assist in a 10-7 loss at Buffalo

Mar. 10 - Reached the 50-goal plateau for the fifth time in his NHL career, beating Bill Ranford in a 6-3 win at Edmonton

Apr. 8 - Tied Wings club record with two shorthanded goals in an 9-1 win at Tampa Bay

Apr. 8 - Led Detroit in goals (58) assists (79) and points (137) for a club-record sixth straight season

Oct. 23 - Suffered herniated disk in neck in collision with Winnipeg's Tomas Steen. Missed 26 games

## 1994

Mar. 4 - Registered 1,100th point of NHL career with a goal against Felix Potvin in a 6-5 loss to Toronto at JLA

June 21 - Underwent surgery to repair herniated disk in neck area

## 1995

| | |
|---|---|
| Dec. 15 - | Recorded 700th NHL assist on a goal by Bob Errey in a 3-1 win over the New York Islanders at JLA |
| Dec. 29 - | Registered 1,200th point of NHL career with an assist in a 2-1 win at Dallas |
| May 27 - | Suffered sprained knee in 6-2 second-round play-off win at San Jose. Missed first three games of Western Conference final series against Chicago |
| June 17 - | Played in first Stanley Cup final game, a 2-1 loss to New Jersey at JLA |
| June 22 - | Scored first Stanley Cup final goal against Martin Brodeur in a 5-2 loss at New Jersey |

## 1996

| | |
|---|---|
| Jan. 25 - | Registered 500th NHL goal against Patrick Roy in a 3-2 win over Colorado at JLA |
| Aug. 26-Sept. 14 | Played for Canada at the first World Cup of Hockey, as the United States defeated the Canadians in a three-game final |
| May 5 - | Tied Wings club play-off record with five points in an 8-3 win over St. Louis at JLA. Also tied club playoff mark with three points in one period |

| | |
|---|---|
| May 8 - | Recorded third Stanley Cup hat-trick against Jon Casey in a 5-4 overtime win at St. Louis |
| May 16 - | Scored the only Stanley Cup overtime goal of his career, beating Jon Casey at 1:15 of the second OT session to give the Wings a 1-0 victory in Game 7 of the Western Conference semifinals against St. Louis |
| Nov. 21 - | Three-point performance in 6-1 win at San Jose moved Yzerman past Alex Delvecchio (1,281 points) into second place on Wings all-time scoring list |

## 1997

| | |
|---|---|
| Jan. 5 - | Registered 1,300th point of NHL career with a goal against Ed Belfour in a 5-5 tie at Chicago |
| Jan. 18 - | Played in NHL All-Star Game at San Jose |
| Feb. 19 - | Played his 1,000th NHL game in a 4-0 shutout of Calgary at JLA |
| Mar. 28 - | Recorded 800th NHL assist on a goal by Larry Murphy in a 2-1 win over Buffalo at JLA |
| Apr. 13 - | Led Detroit in assists with 63 |
| May 31 - | Scored second Stanley Cup final goal against Ron Hextall in his first Stanley Cup final victory, a 4-2 win at Philadelphia |
| June 7 - | Won his first Stanley Cup against Philadelphia, assisting on Darren McCarty's Cup-winning tally in a 2-1 victory at JLA |
| Dec. 31 - | Moved past Alex Delvecchio (825) into second place on Wings all-time assist list with a helper in a 5-2 win against St. Louis at JLA |

## 1998

| | |
|---|---|
| Jan. 28 - | Suffered sprained medial collateral knee ligament in collision with Rick Tocchet. Missed three games. |
| Feb. 7-22 - | Played for Canada in Nagano, Japan as NHLers participated in the Winter Olympics for the first time |

| | |
|---|---|
| Mar. 29 - | Registered 1,400th point of NHL career with a goal against Dominik Hasek in a 4-2 win over Buffalo at JLA |
| Apr. 18 - | Led Detroit in assists (45) and points (69) |
| June 11 - | Scored two goals against Olaf Kolzig as Wings rallied for a 5-4 OT decision over Washington in Game 2 of the Stanley Cup final series at JLA |
| June 16 - | Awarded Conn Smythe Trophy as playoff MVP as the Wings defeated Washington 4-1 at the MCI Center to win their second straight Stanley Cup. Finished as playoff scoring leader and his 18 assists and 24 points equaled Sergei Fedorov's club records |

| | |
|---|---|
| Nov. 11 - | Moved past Bryan Trottier (1,425) into 10th spot on the NHL's all-time points list with an assist in a 6-2 win against St. Louis at JLA |

## 1999

| | |
|---|---|
| Jan. 21 - | Suffered fractured nose and lacerations to face when hit by a Paul Coffey slapshot in game against Carolina. Missed one game |
| Jan. 24 - | Voted a starter on North American team for NHL All-Star Game, but unable to play due to fractured nose |
| Nov. 17 - | Recorded 900th NHL assist on a goal by Brendan Shanahan in a 7-2 win at Vancouver |
| Nov. 20 - | Registered 1,500th point of NHL career with an assist in a 2-1 loss at Edmonton |
| Nov. 26 - | Became 11th NHLer to reach 600 career goals, beating Tommy Salo in a 4-2 win over Edmonton at JLA |
| Nov. 28 - | Joined Luc Robitaille and Brett Hull in starting lineup against Phoenix to make Detroit the first team in NHL history to start a game with three 600-goal scorers in its lineup |
| Apr. 17 - | Led Detroit in scoring with 74 points |
| Apr. 21 - | Recorded fourth Stanley Cup hat-trick, beating Guy Hebert (2) and Tom Askey (1) in a 5-3 win over Anaheim at JLA |

## 2000

| | |
|---|---|
| Feb. 6 - | Played in NHL All-Star Game at Toronto. Voted a starter on North American team |
| Apr. 9 - | Led Detroit in scoring for the 11th and final time with 79 points |
| June 15 - | Awarded Selke Trophy as NHL's top defensive forward |
| June 15 - | Selected as the center on the NHL's First All-Star Team |
| Oct. 16 - | Underwent arthroscopic surgery on right knee. Missed 22 games |

## 2001

**Feb. 23 -** Registered 1,600th point of NHL career with a goals against Brent Johnson in a 4-2 win over St. Louis at JLA

**Apr. 11 -** Left opening playoff game against Los Angeles with a leg injury and missed remainder of playoffs with what was later revealed to be a broken fibula

## 2002

**Jan. 20 -** Recorded 1,000th NHL assist, setting up Mathieu Dandenault for the OT game winner in a 3-2 victory over Ottawa at JLA

**Feb. 24 -** Wins Olympic gold medal as Canada defeats the USA 5-2 in gold-medal game at Salt Lake City.

**Feb. 25 -** Played just one game the rest of the regular season after suffering knee injury in Canada's final Winter Olympic round-robin game against the Czech Republic

**June 13 -** Won his third Stanley Cup as Detroit defeated Carolina 3-1 in Game 5 at JLA to take a 4-1 series victory. Led club in playoff scoring with 23 points. Yzerman and Wings and 2002 Canadian Olympic teammate Brendan Shanahan join Ken Morrow (1980 USA, New York Islanders) as only players to win Stanley Cup and Olympic gold medal in same season

## 2003

**Feb. 24 -** Returned to Wings lineup in 5-4 win over Los Angeles at JLA after missing first 66 games of season following knee surgery

**June 12 -** Awarded Masterton Trophy as the NHL player who best exemplifies perseverance, sportsmanship and dedication to hockey

**Aug. 2 -** Underwent an osteotomy, a bone-realignment procedure, on his right knee. Surgery performed by London, Ont. orthopedic surgeon Dr. Peter Fowler

## 2004

**Jan. 5 -** Recorded 1,024th NHL assist on a goal by Kris Draper in a 6-0 win over Nashville at JLA, surpassing Gordie Howe to become the Red Wings' all-time assists leader

**Jan. 16 -** Registered 1,700th point of NHL career with an assist in a 3-3 tie with Phoenix at JLA

**May 1 -** Suffered scratched cornea and fractured orbital bone when struck by teammate Mathieu Schneider's slapshot during Game 5 of Detroit's second-round playoff series against Calgary

**July 11 -** Selected to Canadian team for 2004 World Cup of Hockey, but unable to play due to eye injury

## 2005

**Aug. 2 -** Following conclusion of NHL lockout, Yzerman signed one-year contract to play his 22nd season with the Wings

**Aug. 15 -** Attended Canadian pre-Olympic camp in Vancouver

**Oct. 13 -** Made his season debut in a 5-2 win at Los Angeles, beginning his record 19th season as captain of the Wings

**Dec. 6 -** Despite a guarantee from Canadian executive director that he'd have a spot on the team, Yzerman bows out of the 2006 Canadian Olympic team, citing that he didn't feel his level of play warranted consideration for the squad

## 2006

**Mar. 21 -** Took the first shootout shot of his NHL career against Nashville's Tomas Vokoun

**Apr. 3 -** Scored the 692nd and final goal of his NHL career against Miikka Kiprusoff in a 2-1 win at Calgary

**Apr. 8 -** Registered the 1,063rd and final assist and 1,755th and final point of his NHL career with a helper on a goal by Jason Williams in a 4-2 win at Columbus

**Apr. 18 -** Played his 1,514th and final regular-season game in a Red Wings uniform in a 6-3 loss at Nashville

**Apr. 21 -** Played in his 20th Stanley Cup tournament as the Wings opened the playoffs with a 3-2 OT win over Edmonton, setting a new club record for most years in the post-season

**May 1 -** Played his 196th and final career Stanley Cup game, registering his 115th assist and 185th point in a 4-3 loss at Edmonton

**July 3 -** Announced his retirement from hockey

**Sept. 25 -** Named vice-president, hockey by Red Wings

**Oct. 5 -** Dropped ceremonial puck between Vancouver captain Markus Naslund and Detroit captain Nicklas Lidstrom at JLA season opener

**Nov. 6 -** Presented Lester Patrick Trophy for outstanding service to hockey in the United States during a luncheon at JLA

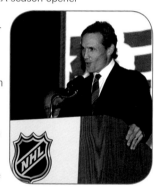

## 2007

**Jan. 2 -** Yzerman's No. 19 sweater is retired in ceremony at JLA prior to game against Anaheim

Photo: Courtesy of the Detroit News

# NINETEEN

## QUICK FACTS

Yzerman collected at least one goal in all of the 21 rinks he played in during the 1988-89 season, the only time in his career he garnered a point in every NHL city.

*Brought To You By:*

**INLAND WATERS POLLUTION CONTROL, INC.**

# Little "Stevie Y"

"If you don't build yourself up, you don't have anything to live up to later. I think Steven understands that as quickly as people can be to jump on your bandwagon, they can be equally as quick to abandon you when things aren't going as well, and that might be a reason why he seems reticent to talk about himself at times. If you continually just lay in the weeds, your words don't come back to haunt you."

*-Ron Yzerman*
on his son's modest nature

"An ordinary person who just likes to get along with people. Just one of the crowd. Nothing extraordinary. That's about it."

*Ron Yzerman*
Steve's father describing
his son's character

"There has been sacrifice on his part. It has taken a lot of hard work for him to get to where he is."

*—Ron Yzerman,*
Steve's father

"Bryan Trottier was my favorite player. As soon as he came into the league, I followed his entire career. In some ways, I tried to play like him. We all have role models and he's mine. In my mind, he's one of the best players ever."

*– Steve Yzerman,*

explaining why he wore No. 19, the same number that Hall of Famer Trottier wore while captaining the New York Islanders to four Stanley Cups from 1980-83.

**OCEAN STATE CLASSIC 1978**
**ALL TOURNAMENT PEEWEE TEAM**
Sponsored By **920 wjar 10 radio-tv**
*Presented By EDGEWOOD RHODE ISLAND HOCKEY ASSOCIATION*

Left to right are Andy Calcione of Edgewood, Roger Mulvenna of Nepean-Canada, Steve Yzerman of Nepean, Jay Octeau of Johnston, and Clark Donatelli of Edgewood. Absent from picture is Paul DeGironimo of Billerica, Mass.

"He was so much more mature than your average 15 year old. It was maturity, his composure and his will to be the best. Everyone of us who played with him that year knew he was going to be something special for a very long time."

*—Darren Pang*
(lower left) Yzerman's teammate on
the Nepean Pirates in 1980-81

"He started here at 16 and you have players up to 20 years of age. He wasn't very big, but he had terrific hockey sense. He didn't have an ego that over-road his ability as a person. He found ways to make his teammates better, and had a knack for putting players -- particularly Bob Errey -- into the clear. Steve is right up there with the top performers that I ever coached and it's hard to find a nicer guy."

— *Dick Todd*
who coached Yzerman at
Peterborough from 1981-83

"When the chips are down, (Yzerman) always made the plays. That's something every leader needs to do, and you have done that."

— *Bill Clinton*
U.S. President

# Welcome to the NHL

# The Early Years

Yzerman comes to the Wings and quickly establishes himself as an NHL star

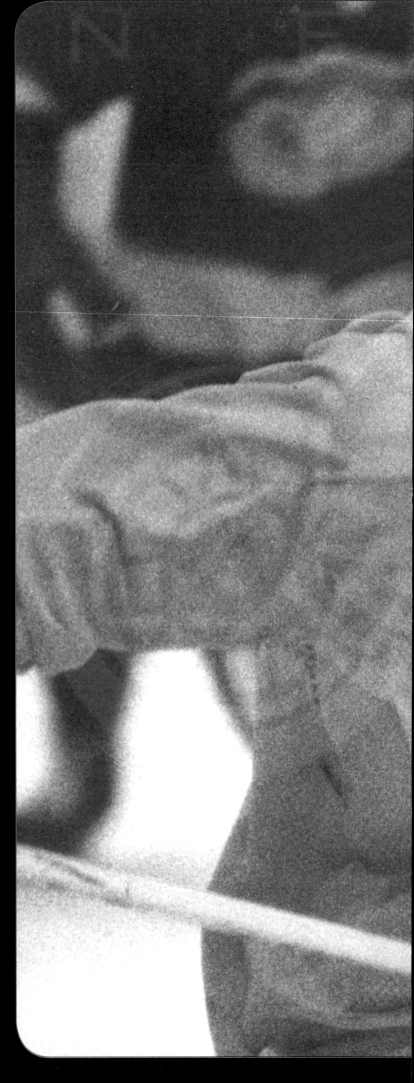

The phenom arrived outfitted with an asterisk.

Steve Yzerman was the fourth player chosen in the 1983 National Hockey League entry draft. The Detroit Red Wings took him, even though he wasn't the player that they coveted most.

"Some of our scouts were disappointed that we didn't get (Sylvain) Turgeon or (Pat) LaFontaine," said Nick Polano, who was Detroit's coach at the time. Turgeon went to Hartford second overall, while local product LaFontaine of Waterford, Mich. was scooped up with the third overall selection by the New York Islanders.

The Wings settled for Yzerman.

It may have been the biggest stroke of good fortune in franchise history.

"There were four players with a lot of acclaim that year," recalled Jacques Demers, Detroit's coach from 1986-90. "We knew we would get one of the four. Steve Yzerman fell to us. A great break for our team."

The Wings were a club floundering amidst a culture of losing. They'd won one playoff series since 1966 up until the point when Yzerman arrived, hardly looking the part of hero.

"Being the head coach, I didn't see him playing junior in Peterborough (with the Ontario Hockey League's Petes)," said Polano, who took over as head coach at the start of the 1983-84 season, Yzerman's rookie campaign. "Jimmy D (Detroit GM Jim Devellano) brought the players in during the summer just before training camp to do strength training and testing. Jim Pengelly was our trainer and he'd come from a soccer background. He was strong on physical training and physical presence, but he really didn't understand hockey players.

"After he'd done all the workouts, he came into my office with the list and gave gave me the reports. He liked (Joe) Kocur, he liked (Stu) Grimson, all the strong guys. And he said, 'You've got one really skinny guy down there, you'll have to send him home. He can't even lift his own weight.' So I said, 'What's his name?' and he said, 'Steve Why-zerman.' And I said, 'No, that's Yzerman and if he can't play, I'm in big trouble as the coach.'"

Everyone would soon learn that it would be the opposition who were in trouble when Yzerman was on the ice.

"The first thing I remember at training camp in Port Huron, I remember saying to (assistant coach) Danny Belisle, 'Let's find out who can play,'" Polano recalled. "'Let's warm up the goalies and have a scrimmage. Let's see who came to training camp in shape and ready to skate.'

"The first thing (Yzerman) did was, he picked up a little pass in the neutral zone and he beat two or three guys and

"When I first came up, I didn't know whether I could even play in the league. So I didn't have any particular goals to shoot for. Just play well and hopefully the points will come."

—Steve Yzerman
about his 500th goal

"Hockey is extremely difficult to give up and he has made an honorable decision to retire and spend more time with his family. He has deservingly gained all the respect from his fans throughout the world. I am proud to have worn the same uniform as he did."

*– Gordie Howe*
NHL Hall of Fame
hockey great

Grosset Sports Library

GORDIE HOWE
by STAN FISCHLER

GORDIE
HOWE

STAN
FISCHLER

The amazing career of
ice hockey's greatest scorer
and most honored player

DUNLAP, Inc.        Publishers        NEW YORK 10010

GROSSET
& DUNLAP
2397

then he beat (veteran defenseman) John Barrett at the blue-line and then went in and pulled Greg Stefan out of the net and top shelfed the puck. I said, 'Holy smokes, who is this guy?'

"Right off the bat, he was our best player. I could see right from the first day that he was going to be a very special player. And when Steve made that big move and scored that goal with everybody watching, I went down to the bench and I said to Pengelly, 'That's that Why-zerman guy.' All the players were just laughing."

That Yzerman dealt so effectively with his detractors at the NHL level was no surprise to those who'd watched him evolve into an NHL player.

"After his family moved here from B.C., I can remember Steve starting to play in our system as a 10-year-old and advancing in a hurry," said Alph May, a longtime manager of minor hockey teams in Nepean, Ont., Yzerman's adopted hometown. "He had a clear sense of anticipation on the ice. He was just a cut above the others. An elite player at every level."

When times were tough, when people doubted him, determination was always Yzerman's closest ally. "There has been adversity," said Ron Yzerman, Steve's father. "He has had his detractors. Too small. Not strong enough. Not mean enough. "It always seemed that whatever Steven did, he had this intensity about him. There was the feeling that he was going to maximize every talent or opportunity he had, no matter what anybody else thought or said."

Mike Goddard, coached Yzerman on bantam, midget, and Tier II junior A clubs in Nepean. "He was a bantam-age player in Tier II junior A," Goddard recollected. "Second-leading scorer in the league as a 15-year-old. The leading scorer was 20."

It was Yzerman's vision that caught Goddard's eye the most. "He saw the ice the way fans see it. Hey, it's easy to figure the game out from the seats. You see all the alleys, all the channels. Steve had that same perspective while he was out there skating."

Polano quickly recognized those traits in his prized youngster as he debuted at hockey's highest level. "He played like the league wasn't hard on him at all," Polano said. "A lot of kids come in and it's a struggle. It's a tough league. It wasn't tough on him to play the game. He just had so much hockey sense and natural ability. When you combine all those skills - skating ability, puck skills, very shifty, hard to hit - what a challenge to stop him. Guys tried to hit him and they couldn't. I'm really proud to tell people that I was his first coach. I gave him a lot of ice time, but he deserved every bit of it, even as an 18 year old.

"When I first saw him, I knew then we had a chance to make the playoffs. And nobody figured we could. But I knew with this guy, we were going to make it. And we did. We made the playoffs two years in a row with him."

Yzerman started strongly and never looked back. "Our first game in Winnipeg, it was a 6-6 overtime tie and he

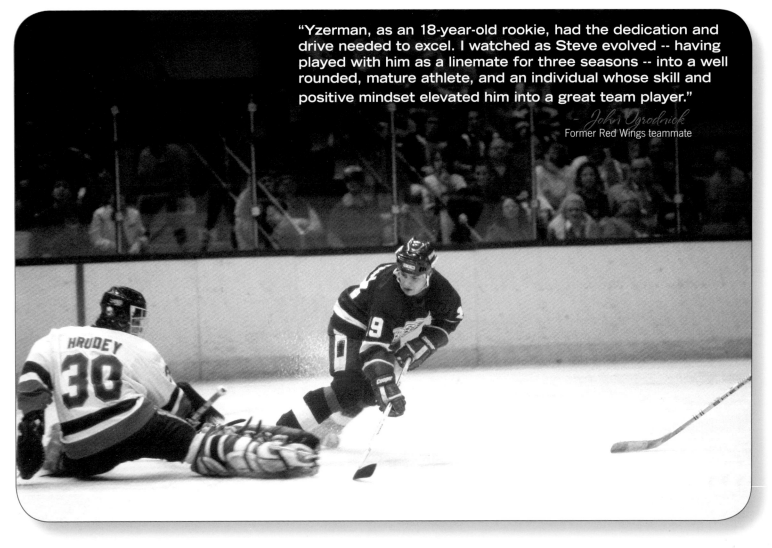

"Yzerman, as an 18-year-old rookie, had the dedication and drive needed to excel. I watched as Steve evolved -- having played with him as a linemate for three seasons -- into a well rounded, mature athlete, and an individual whose skill and positive mindset elevated him into a great team player."

*- John Ogrodnick*
Former Red Wings teammate

scored the tying goal," Polano said. "He beat (Jets defenseman) Bobby Dollas, put it right through his legs and went right around him up the boards and he just scored an unbelievable goal on Doug Soetaert.

"When I started him that game, it was the first game and we didn't want to embarrass the veterans, so we had him playing on the fourth line with Paul Woods and one of the other fellows. After that goal, we said, 'Heck, this guy is going up.' He went from the fourth line up to the first line right off the bat."

Yzerman collected 87 points as a rookie, a Red Wings club record, led the team in scoring and finished second to Buffalo goalie Tom Barrasso in the Calder Trophy voting. The Sporting News named him NHL rookie of the year. "Just watching him through the year, he scored 39 goals that first year at 18 years old and he still could have been playing junior hockey," Polano said. "The most important thing was we made the playoffs that year and he always gave us a chance to win games because he was able to get scoring chances because of his high skill level. When I put him with Ron Duguay and John Ogrodnick, they were a pretty good offensive line in the league. They really clicked."

"He was a baby face and he was so quiet," former Wings goalie Stefan recalled of Yzerman the rookie. "He never said boo, but his talents spoke volumes and he easily made the team out of training camp in 1983. He also quickly made a reputation around the league as an outstanding young player."

As well as things went for him in his early seasons, Yzerman's value only increased due to the passionate fire burning within him, fueling a determination to improve his game.

"He always worked hard, but we were just kids in junior and we liked to go out and enjoy ourselves, too," said Bob Errey, Yzerman's teammate in Peterborough and later in Detroit.

Returning home in the summer months, Yzerman stopped participating in summer shinny outings with many of his childhood friends, insisting they were too enjoyable. "He just explained that hockey was his job and the time had come for him to get serious about it and work harder to make himself better," Goddard remembered.

Polano noticed the change when Yzerman returned to training camp. "He really worked on his strength," Polano said. "He was in that weight room every day and he built up his strength. He became a star in the league at an early age."

The hard times weren't over for the Wings. They suffered through an embarrassing 17-win, 40-point season in 1985-86, leading to the hiring of Demers. But as long as Yzerman was in the lineup, Hockeytown had hope.

"After one practice, we realized he was our best player."

– Jimmy Devellano

# N I N E T E E N
## Q U I C K   F A C T S

Stevie Y wasn't known as a fighter, but he did drop the gloves nine times during his NHL career:

| | | | |
|---|---|---|---|
| Mar. 8, 1984 | Jorgen Pettersson of the St. Louis Blues | Jan. 6, 1988 | Doug Evans of the St. Louis Blues |
| Oct. 13, 1984 | Jan Ludvig of the New Jersey Devils | Dec. 5, 1992 | Rob Ramage of the Tampa Bay Lightning |
| Feb. 2, 1986 | J.F. Sauve of the Quebec Nordiques | Jan. 21, 1993 | Ron Sutter of the St. Louis Blues |
| Feb. 1, 1987 | Doug Smith of the Buffalo Sabres | Apr. 14, 1995 | Chris Chelios of the Chicago Blackhawks |
| Dec. 23, 1987 | Kevin Maguire of the Buffalo Sabres | | |

Yzerman also collected 13 misconducts, six game misconducts and two gross misconducts during his career.

*Brought To You By:*

"I remember being at the first training camp with Steve. I was a minor league goaltender and you knew watching Steve, a few shifts into his first scrimmage, that he would have special talent. I think the greatest qualities that Steve had were his mental abilities, his ability to focus, his competitiveness, his passion, his love for competition and obviously he was the face of the franchise. If he is not the greatest Red Wing of all-time, he and Gordie Howe are certainly the two greatest Red Wings to ever play the game."

– *Ken Holland*
Red Wings General Manager

C

## STEVE YZERMAN

EASTSIDE

topps

"He's given me so many thrills with his hockey. And what he is as a person he gives me joy after joy. I haven't had one bad night from him."

— *Jacques Demers*
former Wings coach

"When I was in my first couple of years, we were starting from the bottom and trying to work toward getting a playoff spot."

*—Steve Yzerman*

"I remember how upset I was when he didn't get rookie of the year when Tommy Barrasso, who had a great year, got it. I felt Steve deserved it and from then on, the way he grew in the league is what impressed me."

*—Doug Weight*
Warren native and St. Louis center

"Through the '80s he really was the franchise. He helped us sell tickets and lure other players here because people wanted to play with him. I think that helped bring Scotty (Bowman) here (in 1993), because he knew Yzerman's abilities and he could see that we were good."

*Jim Devellano*
Detroit Senior Vice-President

Leader
and
Captain

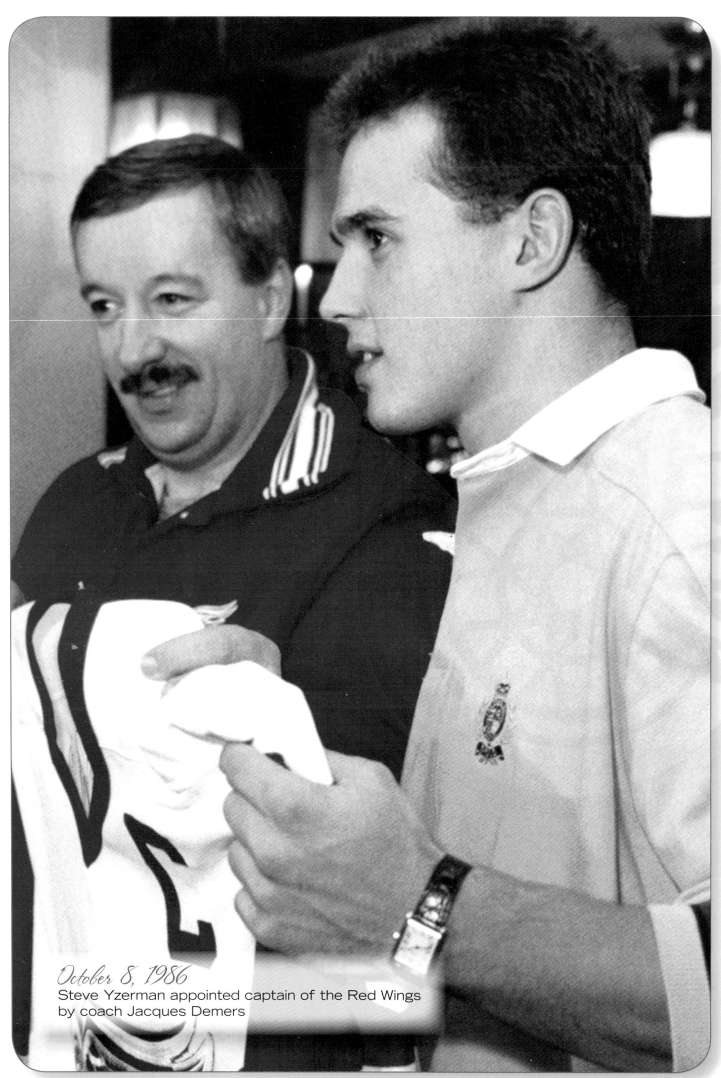

*October 8, 1986*
Steve Yzerman appointed captain of the Red Wings
by coach Jacques Demers

Photo: Courtesy of the Detroit News

"I remember him when he was all bright-eyed and bushy-tailed. When that team needed a lift, he was always the guy they turned to, the one who got them going."

*–Danny Gare*
Detroit's captain
prior to Yzerman

Photo: Courtesy of the Detroit News

# The Leader

Yzerman's role as captain as how his leadership capabilities are looked upon by others.

Despite all his accomplishments, perhaps it's appropriate that the individual outputs of Wayne Gretzky and Mario Lemieux overshadowed Steve Yzerman during their careers, because ultimately, even though his totals look pretty in the yearbook, one was the only digit that interested Stevie Y.

Being on top was always what it was about all about for the captain. His teammates marveled at the unparalleled competitiveness with which Yzerman approached the game.

He was nastier than bipartisan politics. More ornery than the Tasmanian Devil. The captain accepted no passengers on his ship.

Detroit defenseman Chris Chelios, who wore the C with pride for years in Chicago, described Yzerman as, "The ultimate captain. No one competed more than him," Chelios said. "He's been like that ever since I've known him."

A leader by example, Yzerman was never a touchy-feely captain. His sense of humor is biting, his temper explosive. Just ask any NHL official. "I'm sure a lot of referees around the league are doing cartwheels," Yzerman said upon his retirement.

Beloved by Red Wings fans on par with Mr. Hockey, Yzerman shared Gordie Howe's soulless ambivalence towards the opposition.

Yzerman is such a competitor that he admitted he couldn't turn it off when he went home. Card games. Monopoly. Scrabble. It didn't matter. In Yzerman's mind, only one person can be No. 1.

"I have to win at everything," he said. "It's cost me some friends."

Did it ever cost him any sleep?

Hardly.

Yzerman was taking a bullet train to the top and if you didn't want to come along for the ride, he'd gladly arrange a transfer.

"Steve was not that interested in individual honors," former Detroit coach Scotty Bowman said. "He worried about competing, about winning. He didn't take a second off."

Yzerman was 21 when the Wings named him captain prior to the 1986-87 season. When he finally hung up his skates following the 2005-06 campaign, he captained the Red Wings for a National Hockey League record 20 years.

Yzerman was never about fire-and-brimstone speeches. He was always a, "Do as I do," type of leader.

"He was known more for what he didn't say than for what he said," noted Florida Panthers coach Jacques Martin, who coached Yzerman on the 2002 Canadian Olympic team.

Joe Kocur was around when a young Yzerman was named captain of the Red Wings and was also there when

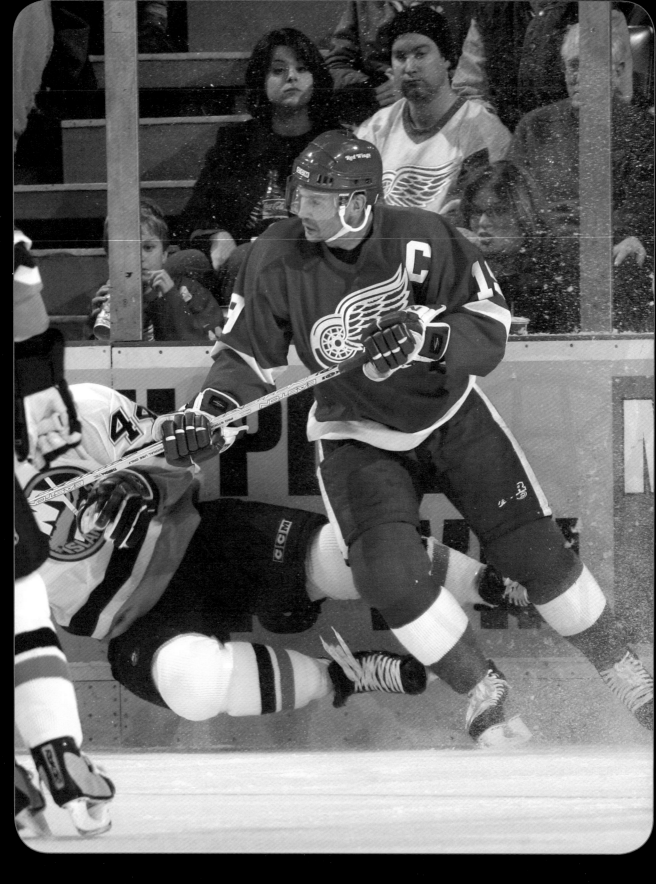

"Steve Yzerman was the ultimate captain. As a player, it would have been an honor for me to have played under his leadership. In addition to his greatness as a player, he also possessed the qualities of being a gentleman – on and off the ice."

–Mathias Norstrom

he led the Wings back to Stanley Cup glory with back-to-back championships in 1996-97 and 1997-98. Kocur felt Yzerman's quiet man status was effective.

"He commanded attention because he was quiet," Kocur said. "He didn't often say things, but when he did, there was a lot of confidence and a lot of meaning behind it. Stevie waited for the right time. He was very calculating about when he was going to talk and what he was going to say."

Former teammate Pat Verbeek summed it up in simpler terms. "He really led on the ice," Verbeek said. "That's where he dominated and he played great all over the ice."

Yzerman was never fond of showboats, of people who weren't genuinely themselves. "I've seen guys light up and thrive on attention," Yzerman said. Added former Detroit teammate Brendan Shanahan, "He doesn't respect people who ham it up . . . who act a different way when the cameras are rolling."

Yzerman sought to downplay the role of captain, believing that what he did wasn't all that spectacular. "I don't think the "C" means as much as people make it out to be,"

Yzerman said. "If you look at any great teams, they don't rely on one player to lead the way."

He took the same approach to the many milestones he achieved during his playing days. As his name moved up to rank amongst the greatest players ever to play the game, Yzerman seemed almost embarrassed to be listed in their class. "It's great to be mentioned in the same sentence with them, but I certainly don't consider myself their equal," he said. "It's hard to place yourself with your heroes - guys who you put way up on a pedestal."

Even on the occasion when he joined the 1,000-point club, Yzerman put the moment on hold, noting he didn't deserve an assist he was credited with during a game against Philadelphia. "I didn't think I deserved it," Yzerman said. "I skated past the official scorer and told him, 'I don't think I touched the puck.'"

In typical Yzerman fashion, he did it quietly, without fanfare. Then, he moved on.

He always left it for others to supply the accolades.

"There were so many intangibles Steve brought to this

team," former Wings coach Dave Lewis said. "Its hard to put his value into words. What he did on the ice, what he did in the locker-room, the players simply enjoyed being around him, even when he was grumpy at times."

Yzerman also bristled at the celebrity status he gained as Detroit's most prominent athlete, such as when a toy company came out with an Yzerman action figure. "All of the Spice Girls have dolls, too," he grumbled. "I don't want to be lumped into that category."

For Paul Woods, who was Yzerman's teammate during his rookie season and viewed the majority of the captain's career from the broadcast booth as Detroit's radio analyst, what make Yzerman a true leader was that he was the consummate professional.

"Obviously, he had the skill of a great player in the National Hockey League, but he also had the work ethic and determination of a grinder and that's what made him so unique," Woods said. "He came into the NHL in the era of Lemieux and Gretzky where without those guys, he was probably the best player in the league. But at the end of the day, when you look at it, he was not only the scorer, of the three, he was the best defensively. Penalty killer? He was the best. Faceoff man? He was the best. In the end, I think he was the best leader of the three. He doesn't always get the notoriety of those two, but really, to me, he goes down as one of the all-time great players of the NHL.

"He got as much satisfaction out of stopping a goal or blocking a shot as he did out of scoring a goal. Not many guys in the NHL have ever been the best offensive player and best defensive player on the same team. Bobby Orr is about the only other one I can think of. It's really a unique thing when you look at it."

Those who played alongside him succinctly understood that unique place that Yzerman held within the game. "It's not just the fans, but we as players were spoiled having him as captain," said Nicklas Lidstrom, Yzerman's successor as Detroit captain.

"The one thing you always knew," Wings center Kris Draper said, "was that through an 82-game season and playoffs, you were going to face adversity. And usually when we faced adversity, Stevie was the guy who stepped up and kind of calmed the waters.

"He was always a calming influence on us and we realize that we don't have that this year."

"We're probably going to look over for the first little while for No. 19," Holmstrom admitted.

"There's definitely a big hole in our hockey club," Draper said. "We've lost the one constant in our team. He knew when he needed to say something. He had such a feel for our team."

"He just played the game that he thought we should all play and led by example," Shanahan said. "That's the best kind of leadership there is."

# N I N E T E E N

## Q U I C K   F A C T S

Alex Delvecchio captained the Red Wings from 1962-73.
Steve Yzerman captained the Wings from 1986-2006.
In between them, 18 different men wore the "C" for Detroit.

**TRAVERSE CITY STATE BANK**

*Salutes Steve Yzerman*

"When it comes to comparing NHL captains, Steve Yzerman is the yardstick by which all others will be judged. He is the penultimate hockey warrior, a player who was willing to do whatever was necessary to win hockey championships. No one in this generation endured more pain in the name of winning than Steve Yzerman."

—Kevin Allen
USA Today hockey writer

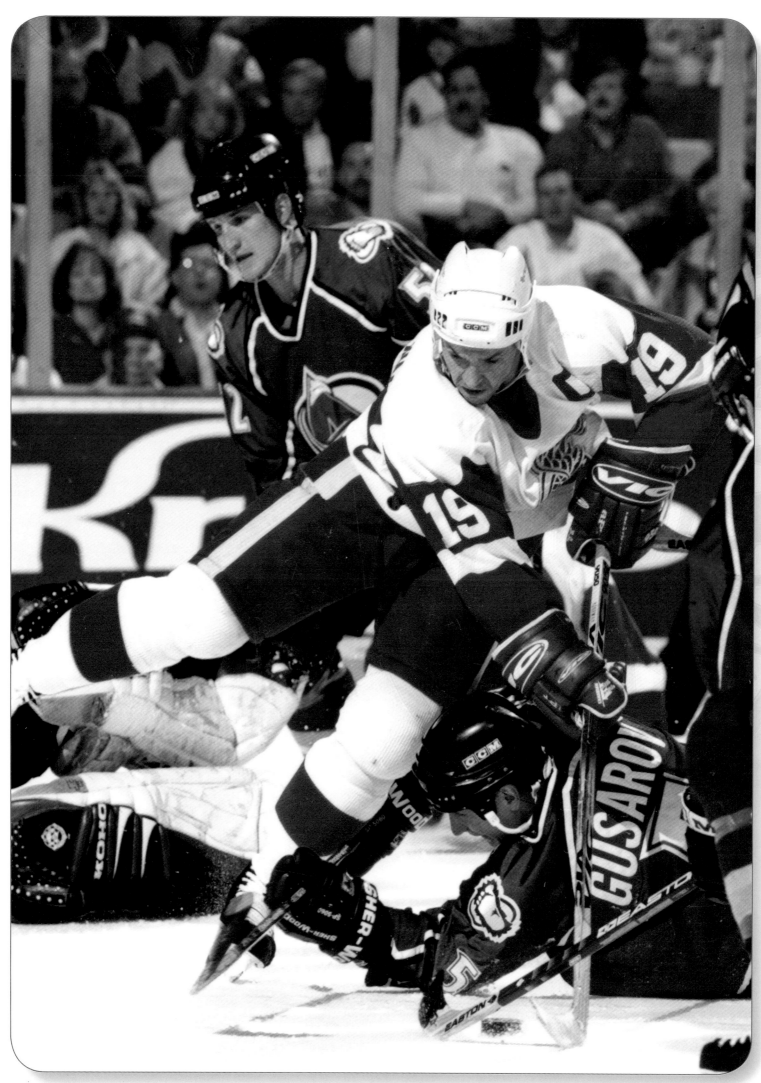

"Steve was a fun, flashy player who was great to watch when he came into the league. Over time you could see how badly he wanted to win and he added other dimensions to his game. He started blocking shots, playing better defense and taking his leadership to a whole other level. He would grind when the game had to be grinded out or score a big, finesse goal when his team needed it. He became a complete player and a complete leader. I witnessed it first-hand playing in Colorado, although I wish I wouldn't have seen it so close. He was a big part of their success and one of the best who's ever played the game."

—*Adam Foote*
Columbus Bluejackets captain

# Eyes On The Prize

# Glory Days

Yzerman establishes himself as a member of the NHL elite and raises the Wings from the depths

Jacques Demers arrived in Detroit in the summer of 1986 with a reputation for getting the most of out his players. He knew he had his work cut out for him with the Red Wings.

He realized he needed a leader. He recognized that there was one already in his lineup.

"I wanted someone with the Red Wings crest tattooed on his chest," Demers said, naming Steve Yzerman his captain. "I knew I had a prized young player and could make the team a different team by naming him captain."

At 21, he was the youngest captain in NHL history, but Demers saw Yzerman as a natural to wear the "C."

"He is dominant both on and off the ice," Demers said. "He's already a great captain. He's playing better now than his first year when he was great coming out of junior. Every time he's out there he's a threat. He's one of the great players of the game, there's no question about it."

Yzerman's contributions on the ice were obvious. He was the best player on the team, its most dominant offensive contributor. "Nobody, absolutely nobody, does as many things for his team as Yzerman does for us," Demers said.

The Wings became a team to contend with during the 1986-87. Demers came up with a defensive system and work ethic that supported Yzerman's offensive prowess and for the first time since the 1977-78 season, the Wings advanced beyond the first round of the playoffs, then rallied from a 3-1 series deficit to defeat the Toronto Maple Leafs in the second round. "We were only a .500 team that year, but we were very competitive," Yzerman said. "Win or lose, we always seemed to be playing one-goal games. I can remember sitting in the dressing room and guys would be saying they just wished we could win one 5-1 for a change. It was funny, because when we got to the playoffs we had that series against Toronto. We were down, and we came back to win it. Every game was tight. It turned out all those close games we played in the regular season helped us when it really mattered."

The Wings took another step forward during the 1987-88 season, finishing first in the Norris Division, their first top-place performance since the 1964-65 season. And Yzerman took another step forward with a personal milestone. Yzerman was 23 the first time he scored 50 goals in an NHL season.

"Before it happened, I didn't think it would mean that much," he remembered. Maybe he was still a little too green to know better. At any rate, his attitude changed at the moment of truth. "I was really excited about it," he re-

"Steve was such a great leader and competitor. Whether it was watching him or playing against him, I always admired his ability to play with great intensity and composure. Steve always seemed to be under control and to lead his team by his strong example on and off the ice."

— Chris Drury
Buffalo Sabres captain

Detroit fell to Edmonton in the Stanley Cup conference finals for the second straight spring. "They probably had the six best players in the world, all in the same lineup," Yzerman said, referring to those Edmonton clubs and the likes of Wayne Gretzky, Mark Messier, Paul Coffey, Jari Kurri, Glenn Anderson and Grant Fuhr. Still, there was no doubt about Yzerman's place in the game. "He's a franchise player, the one guy we are building a team around to win the Stanley Cup," Demers said. "We've made the playoffs two years in a row with Stevie. He's not just a great player on our team, he's a superstar in the National Hockey League. The only thing that bugs me is he doesn't get any votes for the all-star team.

"He does everything for us. I don't know if he can get any better."

Demers would be proven wrong. Yzerman was about to get much better. The 1988-89 season would be a record breaking campaign for him, in terms of individual numbers the best of his NHL career. Yzerman would score 65 goals, dish out 90 assists and those totals, along with his 155 points, were all Detroit records. He won the Lester B. Pearson Award, which is voted on annually by the NHLPA and presented to the member of their brethren they feel has been the best player in the league that season. The Hockey News also named him their player of the year, the first time a Red Wing had won that award since Norm Ullman in 1964-65.

"One thing that's very important to me is how my colleagues and other players think of me," Yzerman said. "I didn't really expect to have the kind of season I had that year, to do the kinds of statistical things I did," he said.

Others weren't nearly as surprised and hockey people were beginning to speak Yzerman's name in the same breath with Wayne Gretzky and Mario Lemieux. Yzerman was not among those people. "I don't ever want to put myself in their category," he stated. "I haven't done the things they've done. I haven't accomplished the things they've accomplished. When they're on the ice, they dominate. That's not the kind of player I am."

The words were hardly surprising. Restraint is Yzerman's trade, understatement his constant companion. "It's pretty much my nature," Yzerman said. "I enjoy living my own life. I want to be part of the community, but not necessarily a figurehead."

Gretzky married an actress. Charlie Simmer married a centrefold. Yzerman married Lisa Brennan, his high-school sweetheart, in the summer of 1989.

"I'm not a movie star," Yzerman said. "I'm not a rock 'n' roll singer. I'm just a hockey player."

One of the best there ever was, it was quickly becoming evident.

# N I N E T E E N
## Q U I C K   F A C T S

Steve Yzerman had six penalty-shot opportunities in his NHL career, scoring on three chances:

| | |
|---|---|
| Nov. 22, 1987 | Doug Kerns, Boston Bruins (no goal) |
| Feb. 13, 1989 | Bob Essensa, Winnipeg Jets (scored) |
| Jan. 3, 1992 | Grant Fuhr, Toronto Maple Leafs (scored) |
| Jan. 29, 1992 | Daren Puppa, Buffalo Sabres (scored) |
| Mar. 18, 1993 | Darcy Wakaluk, Minnesota North Stars (no goal) |
| Nov. 2, 1995 | Blaine Lacher, Boston Bruins (no goal) |

"That's like asking me if I'd trade my son, Jason, for the kid next door."

—Jacques Demers
on talk of Yzerman
being dealt

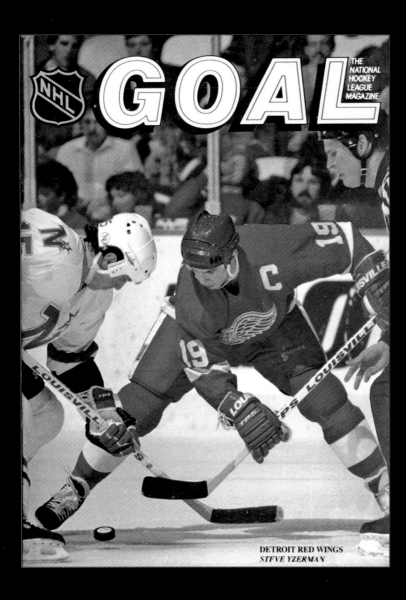

**GOAL**

THE NATIONAL HOCKEY LEAGUE MAGAZINE

DETROIT RED WINGS
*STEVE YZERMAN*

"The first words that come to mind when thinking about Steve Yzerman are respect and intensity. Steven gave everything in a game and some times he gave it back to me. He was such a leader and his desire to win and be so competitive often times throughout our career together would translate into argumentative situations where we both felt that we were doing what we had to do."

—*Kerry Fraser*
NHL referee

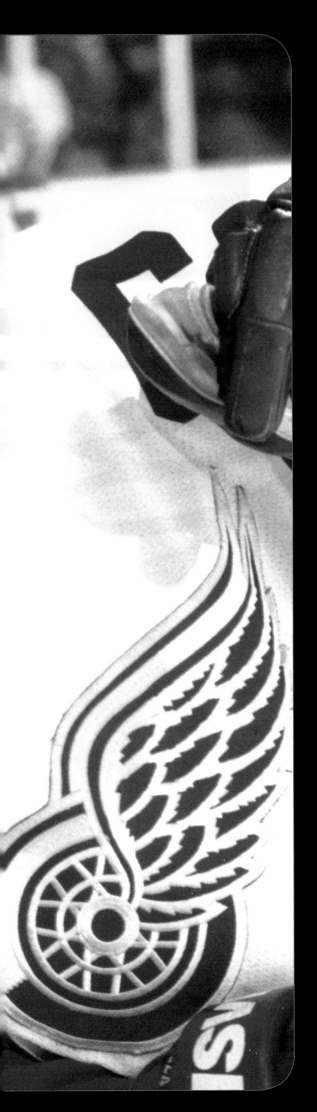

THE OFFICIAL 1991-92 GAME PROGRAM

"The first time I met Steve was at a charity golf tournament when someone introduced him to me. I wasn't in the NHL yet, so he didn't know me. But he talked to me for about 10 minutes as I told him we played for the same Tier II team. To this day he still goes out of his way to say hello, and asks how things are going."

—Adrian Aucoin
—Chicago captain

"The best way to describe Steve Yzerman is that he's a total class act. He is someone that you want to be like, both on and off the ice. He makes everyone around him better people. As a captain, I find myself in situations where I'm trying to emulate him. Not only was he one of the best captains I ever played for, he's one of the best people I've ever known. His greatest quality as a player was that he respected the job everyone on the team had to do. That's because he understands what makes a Stanley Cup champion team."

—Tim Taylor
—Tampa Bay Lightning captain

# Transition Game

Yzerman transforms from offensive dynamo into the total package, combining defense with offense.

The numbers were impressive. The end result was not.

It became a Detroit rite of spring. Steve Yzerman, sweat-soaked, his face encompassed by a barren, pained expression as he sought to explain away another Red Wings playoff failure.

They changed coaches. They switched players. The outcome remained the same.

Detroit missed the playoffs in 1989-90 and made first-round exits in 1988-89, 1990-91, 1992-93 and 1993-94. Eleven years into the league, Yzerman began to wonder if his day would ever come. "It was really embarrassing," Yzerman said of the early playoff exits. "The setbacks make you wonder. You begin doubting yourself."

He remembered trying to get away from it all one spring in Las Vegas, figuring there, of all places, was a location where a hockey player could fly under the radar.

He was at a craps table. A couple of men recognized him. They looked at each other. "We'd better move," the one said to the other. "This table's obviously a loser."

Some suggested that moving Yzerman might be the solution to Detroit's woes.

"We have to see what Steve Yzerman might bring in the market," Detroit coach-GM Bryan Murray said after one early playoff departure. Yzerman's named was linked to deals for Eric Lindros. There were rumors of offers from Washington and the New York Islanders, but Murray ultimately came to his senses.

"If I did that, I might have to leave town," Murray said. "There is absolutely no way. You do not trade a player of Steve's caliber. I've never had a player like him and I intend to keep him. He's been a franchise-type player since he came here and still is. I may be dumb sometimes, but I'm not stupid."

Yzerman was aware of the talk and despite his disappointments in Detroit, didn't view an exit as a solution. "Things haven't been all roses all along here," Yzerman acknowledged. "There have been some difficulties and some differences, but I have no desire to play anywhere else. As far as I am concerned, this is the only place I want to play. I still think I've got a lot of hockey left in me and I still think and expect to win a Stanley Cup in Detroit."

Scotty Bowman, who came to Detroit as coach in 1993, found out just how much Yzerman meant to the team when they were introduced prior to the 1995-96 season opener. Yzerman received a lengthy, thunderous ovation. Bowman, viewed as the perpetrator of recent Yzerman trade talks with Ottawa, was lustily booed.

"Every player enjoys something like that," Yzerman recalled of that ovation. "It's exciting and a thrill for sure. You get a rush. It makes you feel good. It makes you want to play well. It's another moment in my career that stands out."

Bowman, meanwhile, took his reception in stride. "I guess there were a few scattered boos," Bowman remembered with a grin. "It really didn't matter until I looked out on the ice and saw that the players were booing."

Yzerman scoffed at talk that a return to his hometown could boost ticket sales by a couple thousand per game. "The only people I know in Ottawa are my family members and there's only 12 of them," Yzerman said. "That leaves 1,988 tickets unaccounted for."

Certainly, the captain wasn't the one to blame for Detroit's failures. He posted six consecutive 100-point seasons between 1987-88 and 1992-93, collecting at least 50 goals five times in that span. "Steve basically turned this franchise around since the day he came," said Mike Vernon, Detroit's goalie from 1994-97. "There's no doubt that he's a superstar."

Yzerman was also evolving in his role as captain, although he downplayed his leadership role on the Wings. "As time goes by, I'm feeling more and more comfortable with the role," he said. "I still don't have a lot to say. I don't feel I have to. Everybody here is fairly intelligent. A captain shouldn't have to tell somebody how to do a job."

Some nights, though, Yzerman wondered aloud whether the commitment was there for the Wings to go all the way. "The line between winning and losing is playing hard, the intensity," Yzerman said. "Every team's success is measured by how it fares in the playoffs. We talk about being a good team. But everybody has to ask themselves, 'Do we want to win on a regular basis?'"

Yzerman did. And he was ready to do whatever it took, even if it meant completely altering his own game. He was willing to forego the 100-point seasons, the glamor and the numbers, in exchange for the only digit that mattered - the chance to be No. 1.

"When you first come into the league, you want to make your mark individually and Stevie did that," said Boston Bruins coach Lewis, a teammate of Yzerman's during those early years in Detroit and later his coach. "Through the years, you learn that to win and be successful, you have to be a more all-around player. He saw that and we reaped the rewards because of it. Stevie turned into the complete package."

"Players like Steve carry the weight of the world on their shoulders," added Bowman. "He was trying to do it all here. But as the team has gotten better, (Yzerman's) done more. He's a solid, two-way player. He's scored more goals and a lot of points, but those years Detroit didn't do much. They went on the attack all the time. I think he enjoys the defensive side of the game and he can contribute."

Bowman felt he'd coached a player similar to Yzerman during his days winning five Stanley Cups behind the bench of the Montreal Canadiens. "I like to compare him to Jacques Lemaire," Bowman said. "In the early part of his career, they said all he could do was shoot. Then he started killing penalties and by the end of his career, he was the best two-way player in the league."

"Well, obviously growing up in Michigan, he was an idol and a guy that I watched very closely. He was the star in Detroit and did so many great things for the organization and for Hockeytown. He basically built Hockeytown from the ground up almost, and he was a guy that you would watch and try to emulate as a young player. He's classy individual as well."

*—Brian Rolston*
Minnesota Wild captain

"Nobody can disagree that every time he stepped on the ice he left everything on it. He was one of the best leaders in hockey, if not in sports. He led by example and he really sacrificed everything for the team. That's why he will be a hall of famer and he's going to be respected all over the world and remembered for that."

*—Zdeno Chara*
Boston Bruins captain

Yzerman found the transition from offensive dynamo into double-duty performer quite satisfying. "For me to be scoring less, it wasn't personally troubling at all," he said. "We were all asked to put defense first on the ice."

That the Wings reached the 1995 Stanley Cup final against the New Jersey Devils only served to show that the change had done them good. "We had a good playoff run," Yzerman remembered. "The most exciting part of it was being in the finals. Once you get there, you find out in a hurry you've got to be ready."

In their first Stanley Cup final since 1966, the Wings were unceremoniously swept aside by the Devils, but the result propelled their turnaround in a 1995-96 campaign that saw them win an NHL-record 62 games, leading to a playoff which would feature Yzerman's most magical individual moment in Stanley Cup competition.

Trailing the St. Louis Blues 3-2 in the second round, Yzerman worked doggedly as a checker to silence the offensive talents of Blues stars Wayne Gretzky and Brett Hull, while providing the offensive spark that would put the team over the top.

Yzerman's tally at 1:15 of the second overtime period, the only playoff OT goal of his career, gave Detroit a 1-0 win over St. Louis and victory in the seventh and deciding game of their Western Conference semifinal series. "It was a blood and guts goal," said Red Wings owner Mike Ilitch, who suffered through the years of despair with his captain. "This one tops it all, because of the way it evolved. Stevie just put his head down and put every ounce into it."

St. Louis captain Gretzky had tried to intercept Vladimir Konstantinov's clearing pass, but couldn't control it. Yzerman pounced on the elusive disc and brought it across the St. Louis blueline, drilling a shot into the top of the net past Blues goalie Jon Casey. "I don't usually shoot from there," recalled Yzerman, who grabbed the puck as a memento of his accomplishment. "I didn't get much speed going through the neutral zone, so I figured I'd just shoot and see what happens."

The emotion of that comeback sapped the strength from the Wings and they fell in six games to the eventual Stanley Cup champion Colorado Avalanche in the Western Conference final.

Another heartbreak in Hockeytown.

"It was supposed to be the breakthrough year for us," Yzerman recollected. "We got past the first round of the playoffs (in 1995) and we lost in the finals. This was going to be the season. We were going to go back to the playoffs and go all the way to win the Stanley Cup.

"The setbacks made you wonder. I was getting tired of hearing how good the Detroit Red Wings were."

The hockey world was also beginning to wonder whether time was running out on the captain, but he'd soon find out that his time had finally arrived.

"I really think Steve is one of the greatest leaders in sports. He led by example. He had tremendous talent, but he really worked for it. I saw him on and off the ice and the way he carried himself. As an athlete, he is the type of person that you want to follow, plain and simple."

*–Rod Brind'Amour*
Carolina Hurricanes captain

"His offensive talents speak for themselves, but the thing that sticks out in my mind from playing against him is how he would do the little things, like go down to block a shot or stand in there and take the hit to try to get the puck out of the zone to get an offensive opportunity. Those are the things you have to do to have success in hockey, and when you see one of your best offensive players doing those things, it's pretty inspiring."

—Scott Niedermayer
Anaheim Ducks captain

"I played against him a lot of years. There were a lot of wars between Colorado and Detroit. He was a great player and it was very tough to play against him. He was always an honest player who played hard. He was a class act who won a lot of cups there in the end. I wish him all the best and good luck in the future. It was great to play against him."

*Peter Forsberg*
Philadelphia Flyers captain

"Few players in the game are respected more than Steve Yzerman. He was an outstanding player who had a tremendous influence on his teammates and the game. I had the opportunity to meet him through Hockey Canada and was impressed with his presence on and off the ice. He was the ultimate leader, a winner, and the consummate professional. I am proud to say I played against him and I wish him all the best."

—*Shane Doan*
Phoenix Coyotes captain

"I've got a bit of a temper. I don't like guys taking a shot at me and I'll back myself up. I won't hurt anyone. I'm not a big and strong guy, but I won't back down. It's important to play hard. If not, you can be intimidated. (If you're intimidated), it gives them confidence, and I'm not going to give anybody an edge over me."

—*Steve Yzerman*
Commenting on his mean streak

Photo: Courtesy of the Detroit News

"Steve was an incredibly skilled player that was tough to play against at both ends of the ice. His play on the ice and the way he conducted himself away from the rink showed players and fans that he has great respect for the game."

—Mats Sundin
Toronto Maple Leafs captain

# N I N E T E E N
## Q U I C K   F A C T S

The 1999-2000 season was a milestone season for Yzerman. He tallied his 600th goal and collected his 900th assist and 1,500th point. As well, he assisted on the 500th career goal by Pat Verbeek and the 300th career goal by Sergei Fedorov.

"Steve Yzerman was a tremendous hockey player who epitomized everything good about our game. He loved the game and played with passion every night. He was a winner who led Detroit to three Stanley Cups and was always there for his country to represent Canada on the international stage. He was the face of the Detroit Red Wings and will be remembered as one of the best players and leaders that ever played the game of hockey. It was a pleasure to have worked with him."

*—Wayne Gretzky*
Phoenix Managing Partner
and Head Coach

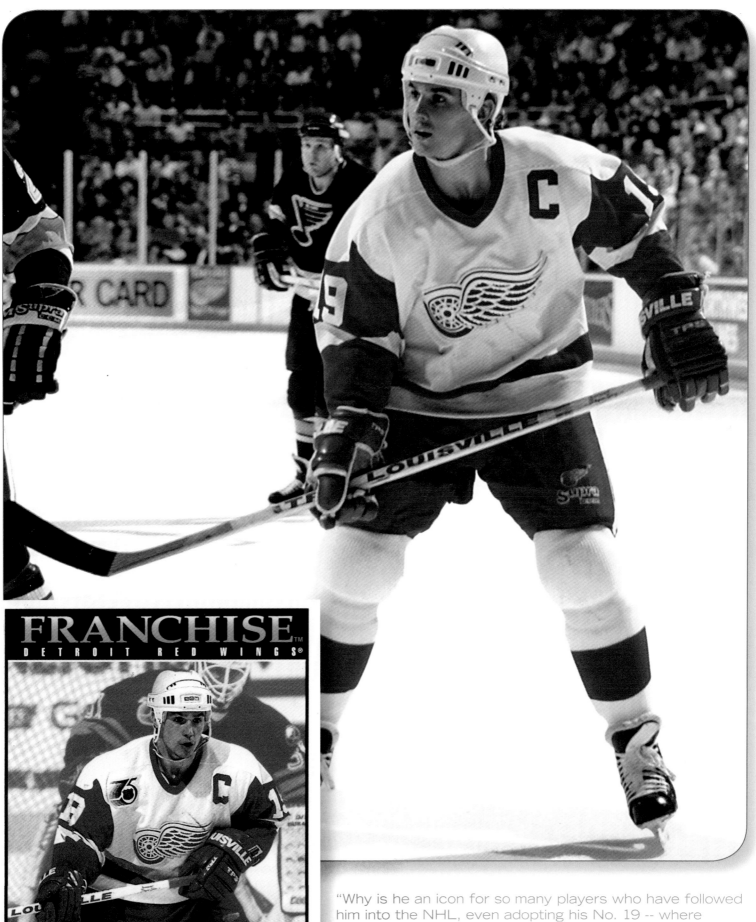

FRANCHISE™
DETROIT RED WINGS®

STEVE YZERMAN

SCORE®

"Why is he an icon for so many players who have followed him into the NHL, even adopting his No. 19 -- where available -- as theirs?  Answer: passion and commitment for his team, his teammates, and his own contribution to both. That's what I read from the intensity on that face once the clock was moving. As kids, that's what we read major leaguers were about. That's why the No. 19s and the respect for Steve Yzerman."

—Mike Emrick
veteran NHL broadcaster

# Stanley Cup Champion

"The fans of Detroit, the players, the world knows that this is Hockeytown. One current player...one current player has been captain of his team longer than any other NHL player today. Its' my pleasure to present the Stanley Cup to Steve Yzerman."

— *Gary Bettman*
NHL Commissioner

It was midway through the 1996-97 season and the Detroit Red Wings were floundering. Less than a season removed from a National Hockey League-record 62 wins, it looked to many in the game that Detroit's window of opportunity to win a Stanley Cup was closing quickly.

The captain disagreed.

"I'm encouraged about our chances," Steve Yzerman said. "I feel a lot more excitement on this team. Physically, we're much bigger on the wings. We're positioned in more of a playoff mode."

In 13 seasons as a Red Wing, Yzerman had lived through enough playoff heartache to break any man. There were debilitating injuries. Devastating defeats.

First-round losses to eighth-seeded teams. Colossal failures. The Wings were destiny's disasters and Yzerman was their poster boy. If good things did come to those who wait, fate owed Yzerman big time.

A trip to the precipice of glory in 1995 appeared to remove the hex, but the door was slammed in their faces by the New Jersey Devils in a four-game sweep during Detroit's first visit to the Stanley Cup final since 1966. "It all happened so quickly, I don't think we had time to get frustrated," Yzerman remembered of that 1995 setback.

The face of the Red Wings, he felt those failures more than anyone, forced to stand up each spring and explain away another devastating demise. It impacted how Yzerman lived his life in the Motor City.

"When you don't win, you end up just beating yourself up," he said. "You don't want to go out. You don't want to be recognized. You put your hat on, you put your sunglasses on. You walk around in a shell almost, because you're embarrassed."

So strong was his desire to sip champagne from Lord Stanley's mug, Yzerman completely altered his game, modifying an up-tempo offensive star into a two-way performer. Teammates took notice of his personal sacrifice for the betterment of the club. "Keeping the goals against down has been the focus here and a key to doing that has been the ability of players such as Stevie Yzerman to change his style of play," defenseman Bob Rouse said. "He had to buy into what the coaches were trying to implement and he's done that, which is a big reason why we've been successful."

Added Brendan Shanahan: "I think the reason why we were successful was because in the dressing room guys got recognized for little things that maybe you're not getting praised for in the papers. That's what Stevie started. He was the first guy that kind of made sacrifices to play a different game. He changed his style for (Wings coach) Scotty (Bowman) and the whole team followed suit."

For Yzerman, altering his game was made easy for him by the demands of Bowman. "We were told that was the way it was going to be and if you wanted to get on the ice you had to play well defensively," Yzerman said. "In that sense, it was pretty easy to adapt. And I think the change in the way I play has had a real positive effect on my career. I like the style of hockey I'm playing now more so than how I was playing five years ago. I produced more offensively before but what did our team ever win?

"Our club has a lot more depth now. If one line doesn't score, you know another line is going to go out and score." Bowman understood succinctly that Yzerman was the key to getting the team to buy into his system. "Steve Yzerman has been here through it all," Bowman said. "It starts with him." The Wings built a new type of team, one with more size, one that was more in your face, tougher to play against. A play-off-style squad. "The complexion of our team definitely changed," Yzerman recalled.

When the playoffs started, panic quickly set in. The Wings were shutout by St. Louis in the first-round opener and didn't score until the third period of Game 2, but they rallied to win that game and take the series in six. Anaheim was shunted aside in four games, bringing on a rematch with Colorado in the Western Conference final.

It was no contest. The Wings took a six-game decision in a series that wasn't nearly that close. They were going back to the Stanley Cup final to meet the Philadelphia Flyers. "I never lost the belief that I'd get another chance," Yzerman said of this Stanley Cup shot.

It was no shot in the dark. The series started in Philadelphia and the Wings took both games. A 6-1 rout in Game 3 at Joe Louis Arena set the stage for a Detroit party. Darren McCarty scored what would prove to be the Cup winner in a 2-1 decision in the clincher, on a feed from the captain. For the first time since 1995, the Cup would reside in Hockeytown. Yzerman finally had the elusive championship to add to his Hall of Fame resume.

"It's the only accomplishment that really matters," Yzerman said. "By far, the most rewarding thing is going through four rounds of the playoffs and winning the Stanley Cup."

He endured the heartache and found out it was worth the wait. That nagging question about whether he and the Wings had what it takes to win could no longer be posed. "Until you win, you always hear, 'Does this player or does that team have what it takes to win?'" Yzerman remembered. "There was definitely a change in perception not only of myself but our entire organization after us winning the championship."

Yzerman watched with delight as the normally stern-faced Bowman donned his skates to take his own turn around the ice with Lord Stanley's mug, his eyes filled with the glee of a child. "That was great wasn't it?," Yzerman said, "To see him excited. To see him smiling. He doesn't let people get too close, he doesn't show his emotion except when he's mad. For a few minutes there, he was one of us."

The years of pain and disappointment now a distant memory, Yzerman was living the fantasy. "For as long as I can remember, I've dreamed of lifting the Stanley Cup," Yzerman said. "I watched the presentation every year, I watched the dressing-room celebration and dreamed of the day it would be me. I don't know if you can ever equal a dream, but this was pretty close. It was a weird sensation. I couldn't wait for the game to be over, but at the same time, I didn't want it to ever end."

N I N E T E E N

"For as long as I can remember, I dreamed of lifting the Stanley Cup. I watched the presentation every year. I watched the dressing-room celebration and I dreamed of the day when it would be me."

*—Steve Yzerman*

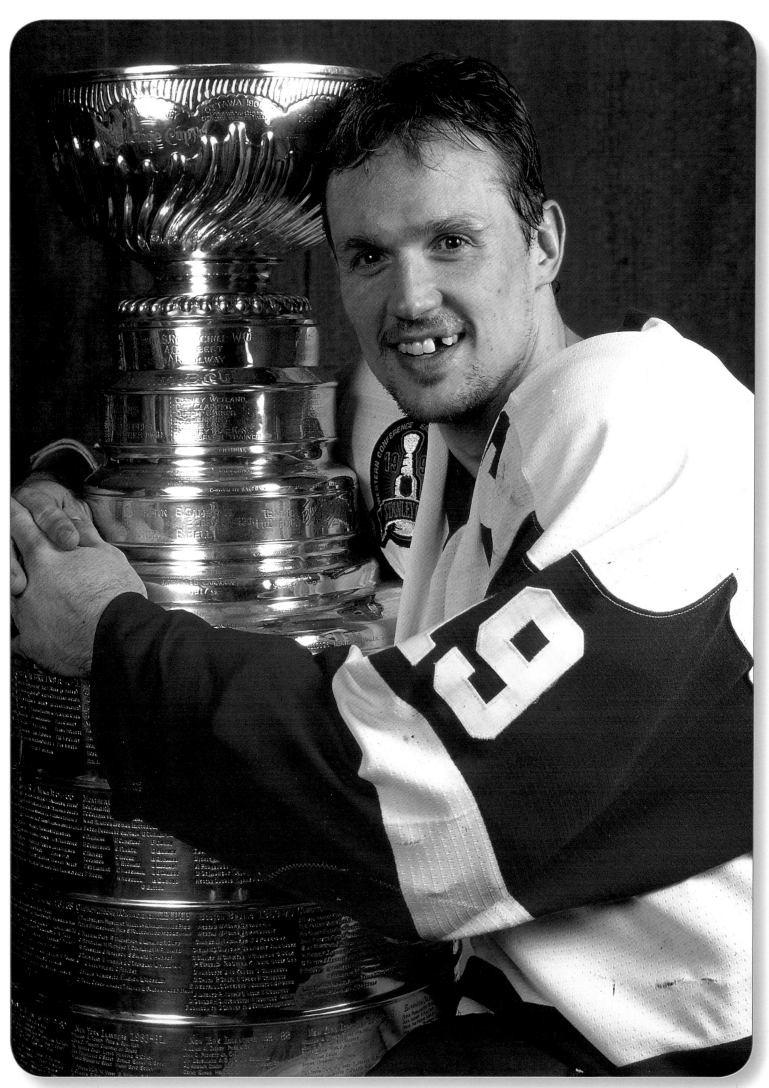

Led by their captain, the Wings pull together after an unspeakable tragedy to
retain the title

It was supposed to be a joyous occasion. The party was
going to last all summer.

In reality, it didn't make it through the first week.

Six days after their 1997 Stanley Cup triumph over the
Philadelphia Flyers, the Red Wings gathered for a golf out-
ing, a last chance to embrace their accomplishment before
going their separate ways for summer.

Not wanting anything to go wrong, players rented limou-
sines to take them home. One limo carried Wings defensemen Viacheslav Fetisov and Vladimir Konstantinov and
team masseuse Sergei Mnatsakanov.

They never made it home.

The limo went out of control and crashed into a tree.
Both Mnatsakanov and Konstantinov suffered debilitating
brain injuries. Fetisov recovered from his injuries and returned to the Red Wings blue-line.

Many in hockey wondered how the Wings would ever
recover from the setback.

"Vladdy had developed into one of the best defensemen in the league," Yzerman said. "The accident was devastating. It was just a sickening feeling. We knew we really
wouldn't know how the team would react to the situation
until we got out on the ice."

Yzerman saw to it that the Wings retained their composure, that they remained a team and overcame their emo-
tional scars. From the moment they arrived for training
camp, he was on top of the situation. "I think the atmosphere is similar to what was going on last year," he said at
the time. "I think our attitude and the way we are approach-
ing things is similar to last year."

The season started with a western road trip and in Edmonton, Yzerman paused to admire the many Oilers Stanley
Cup banners hanging from the rafters of the Northlands
Coliseum, knowing that in a few day's time, he'd be seeing
such a banner raised to the rafters at Joe Louis Arena.

"All the years looking at the banners in the other team's
rinks, wondering what it would be like to have one of our
own," Yzerman remembered. "It's not that we didn't have
any banners hanging up there. It's just that there was this
gap . . ."

During the season, Yzerman set the tone for the Wings
by doing it all on the ice. "He blocks shots, he battles with
big defensemen," Wings assistant coach Dave Lewis said.
"You would like a guy like Steve Yzerman to be with you in a
battle on the ice or a back alley."

Wings coach Scotty Bowman marveled at Yzerman's
unparalleled dedication. "He's one of the players, and there
are few, who come to work every day," Bowman said. "You
kind of have to shoo him off the practice ice."

"...and now lets talk about Hockeytown. This is a great team, a great organization. Steve Yzerman, lets do it again, come get the Stanley Cup."

*— Gary Bettman*
NHL Commissioner

The respect and admiration Yzerman was receiving around the league was ramped up to another level, but he scoffed at the notion that just because he'd lifted a Stanley Cup, he'd become a better player. "If you play well and win, you're a heck of a leader; you don't win and you're an OK leader and if you don't play well and you don't win you're a lousy leader," Yzerman said.

During the 1997-98 season, Yzerman was the unquestioned leader of the Red Wings, even if he chose to continue to question that role himself. "Scotty Bowman is the leader of our team," Yzerman suggested. "In my opinion, I don't do a whole lot."

All he did was lead the Red Wings to their second consecutive Stanley Cup and pick up the Conn Smythe Trophy as the most valuable player in the playoffs in the process. As was his style, Yzerman preferred to place the credit for Detroit's success elsewhere. "That was a statement more so of the team as a whole," he said of the back-to-back Cup triumphs. "I think the team had gotten to a point where we didn't care about stats."

Yzerman's totals in the regular season during the 1997-98 season were among his lowest in a very productive career. The same guy who scored 65 goals for the Wings in 1988-89 tallied just 69 points this season.

That was the lowest total to lead the Stanley Cup champion in scoring during a full season since Jean Beliveau had 68 points for the 1967-68 Montreal Canadiens. Beliveau, like Yzerman, was a long-serving captain, well-respected by his peers, but whose individual accomplishments were often overshadowed by the likes of Gordie Howe and Bobby Orr.

In Yzerman's era, he often took a back seat to Wayne Gretzky and Mario Lemieux. "He played all his career in their shadows," Bowman said. "Steve was not that interested in individual honours, though. He worried about competing, about winning."

The route to Lord Stanley's mug followed a journey similar to Detroit's 1997 triumph. The Wings were forced to rally to take out the Phoenix Coyotes in the first round, then disposed of the St. Louis Blues in Round 2. The Dallas Stars, who'd defeated Detroit for the Central Division title during the regular season, were felled in the Western Conference final.

The Eastern Conference champion Washington Capitals awaited in the Stanley Cup final, but just as in 1997, it was no contest. The Wings swept the Caps aside in the minimum four games.

Yzerman credits his experience with the Canadian Olympic team at the 1998 Winter Games in Nagano, Japan, for putting a revitalizing charge into his game as Detroit headed toward the post-season that year.

"There are times when you doubt yourself as a player," he admitted. "Getting out there, playing with and against the

elite players of the world, it proved to me that I still belonged at that level."

The change was noticeable. Yzerman's 18 assists and 24 points during that spring equaled Detroit club playoff records. "Since he came back from the Olympics, he has been a bit of a different player," said winger Joe Kocur, an Yzerman teammate since the mid-1980s.

"He has totally controlled our hockey team and everything that we have done.
"I don't know what happened over there - must have been the water or something - but we are going to have to send him back there in the summer."

As the players paraded with the Cup for the second consecutive spring, Konstantinov, in a wheelchair, joined the festivities on the ice and the emotion of the players was palpable.

As much as there was joy at the outcome, for Yzerman, there was melancholy in seeing his former teammate unable to be part of it all. "It's been a physically and emotionally-draining season that just never seemed to end," Yzerman said. "As happy as I am to win, I'm equally happy that it's over."

As he spoke at the Stanley Cup parade in Hart Plaza a few days after the title was won, Yzerman recognized the efforts of this team that had overcome such a terrible loss.

"In 14 years here in Detroit, I played on almost 14 different teams, it seems," he said. "This is the closest group of players, the most unselfish group of players, the hardest-working, most dedicated team I've ever been a part of."

Steve Yzerman
1998 STANLEY CUP CHAMPION

N I N E T E E N

# 2002 Stanley Cup

**A severely injured captain endures the pain and carries Detroit to another championship**

Steve Yzerman shared his ordeal in vivid detail.

Every grimace, every anguished stride, captured by the lens.

On the ice, the captain of the Detroit Red Wings wasn't anywhere near the all-star player he'd been during a Hall of Fame career. By the time the Wings reached the Stanley Cup final against the Carolina Hurricanes, he was so severely hampered by an injured knee that his value existed solely as a faceoff man and penalty killer. He contributed one goal during his last 13 playoff games.

Off the ice, though, he was never better.

"He's the best leader I've ever seen," expressed Luc Robitaille, a 16-season NHL veteran, but a first-year Red Wing that season.

Yzerman was never a gung-ho guy. When he did speak, the message was clear.

Moments after Detroit took a 3-1 lead in the Cup final set, Yzerman stepped up to his impromptu podium in the Wings' dressing room. He realized there were two off days before Game 5 in Detroit and that the city would be bubbling with enthusiasm over the impending Cup verdict. He knew this was a dangerous equation.

Photo: Courtesy of the Detroit News

His advice to his teammates? Don't talk to anyone. Don't answer the phone. Ignore the doorbell.

Keep the focus on winning Game 5.

"He had that team ready for the next game the instant they won Game 4," remembered NHL analyst and former Chicago Blackhawks goalie Darren Pang, Yzerman's closest friend. "He was in complete control the entire playoffs. It was a magnificent performance."

A performance rendered all the more amazing, considering what Yzerman endured daily to keep himself in the game.

His right knee, surgically repaired earlier in the season, was reinjured during the 2002 Winter Olympics as he helped Canada win the gold medal, but Yzerman kept playing, determined to gain gold for Canada.

Mission accomplished, he returned to Detroit and received the bad news - his knee was an absolute mess. He rested it the remainder of the regular season, playing just once in preparation for the playoff run.

Everyone - Yzerman included - worried whether he'd be able to survive the grind. "We wondered whether we were even going to have Stevie in the lineup," Detroit center Kris Draper recalled. "He had some really horrible practices and was really struggling."

"Players said, 'As long as he can suit up, we can win,'" Detroit coach Scotty Bowman recalled. "And he did more than suit up."

Acknowledging the pain, but refusing to be overwhelmed by it, Yzerman persevered. He never missed a shift, let alone a game, leading the Wings by example, as well as in playoff scoring with 23 points, in the process, surpassing Gordie Howe as Detroit's all-time playoff scoring

"...Steve Yzerman come get it."

leader. "He was a true leader for us to follow," Detroit defenseman Nicklas Lidstrom said. "He showed a tremendous commitment in the playoffs, playing through injury, through pain."

That was a season in which everyone expected the Wings to walk away with the title. During the off-season, Robitaille and Brett Hull were signed as free agents, joining Yzerman to give the Wings three 600-goal scorers, an NHL first. Two-time Hart Trophy winner and six-time Vezina Trophy winner Dominik Hasek was acquired a trade with Buffalo to play goal.

Some dared to suggest that the 2001-02 Wings might be the best assemblage of hockey talent ever witnessed in one NHL dressing room. "You walk in here and it's just like being at the all-star game," Robitaille.

The captain made certain no one performed like it was the all-star game. "If you're content with sitting on the bench, then I guarantee you that a guy like Steve Yzerman doesn't want you around," Hull said.

Some in the game wondered how the Wings would get along with so many superstars in tow, but the captain was quick to squelch such talk. "People make too much out of chemistry," Yzerman suggested. "You can hate a guy, but as long as he comes to the rink and does his job every day, that's all that matters."

The Wings got along just fine, steamrolling their way to the President's Trophy and making short work of Anaheim and St. Louis in the first two rounds of the playoffs. But in the Western Conference final, the Colorado Avalanche had other ideas, taking a 3-2 series lead with a Game 5 overtime win at Joe Louis Arena. The Wings gutted out a victory at the Pepsi Center to force Game 7 and it was no contest. The Wings were 7-0 winners.

"Getting four (goals) in the first (period), you couldn't have planned it better," Yzerman remembered. "But the fifth goal, we all looked at each other, it was huge. It took the life right out of them. We had been prepared to go to overtime or a 1-0, 2-1 game. We were as surprised as anyone."

Almost as surprised as the Wings were to face the Hurricanes for the Cup. Carolina scored an OT verdict in Game 1, then the Wings swept four in a row.

When it was over, Yzerman brought his children to ice level to live the celebration with him and held hands with his oldest daughter Isabella as they came out together to accept Lord Stanley's mug from NHL commissioner Gary Bettman. "This is maybe the most enjoyable year I've had in hockey," Yzerman said, reveling in the celebration of Detroit's third championship in six years. "(2002) was a pleasant surprise, to understate a little bit. It was like, 'This is awesome, I'd like to do this one more time. I'll never get tired of doing this.'"

N I N E T E E N

Photo: Courtesy of the Detroit News

"The Stanley Cup is such a journey. You've got the regular season, then four rounds of playoffs. Once you win it, the emotion of the accomplishment just explodes from within you."

– *Steve Yzerman*

# N I N E T E E N
## Q U I C K   F A C T S

Such was the respect for Yzerman around the NHL that during the 2004 World Cup of Hockey, which Yzerman missed due to an eye injury, both Joe Sakic and Joe Thornton, who regularly wear No. 19 for their NHL teams, refused to take the sweater number out of respect for Yzerman.

*Thanks For The Memories*

# The Captain in the Community

Through all the accolades, the litany of accomplishments, the never-ending run of excellence, one factor continues to make Steve Yzerman stand out from the crowd.

His down-to-earth modesty.

When Yzerman was setting records and surpassing legends as captain of the Detroit Red Wings, he seemed almost embarrassed to be putting some of his boyhood idols in the rear-view. In the same fashion, he downplays the charity work he's performed during his 23 years with the team.

"I don't know that I've done a whole lot," Yzerman suggests when queried about his community work. "I've been in Detroit for a long time and I know a lot of people. When I've been available, I've just tried to show up and help out, rather than set up any sort of foundation."

As he always did when the subject came around to his on-ice exploits as one of the greatest players ever to skate in the National Hockey League, Yzerman prefers to leave the accolades to others.

Ron Giles is an office worker in Windsor and also someone who donates bone marrow to aid with seriously ill people. Through his own charity work, Giles came to meet Tom Garrett, a teenager from Peterborough, Ont. suffering from acute myeloid leukemia and also graft-versus-host disease, a condition where the donated bone marrow attacks the body.

Yzerman is Garrett's favorite NHL player and Giles made it his mission to arrange a meeting between Garrett and Stevie Y. He didn't know how easily such a request would be met, but that's only because he didn't know Yzerman.

Through the assistance of former NHLer John Druce, the Wings were contacted and the meeting was arranged last October when the Wings were in Calgary to play the Flames. Garrett was in Calgary getting treatments for his illness at the time. "You

could just see the smile on his face grow big," Giles said of Garrett's meeting with the Detroit captain. "We were all thrilled.

"He told me he always wanted to meet Steve Yzerman."

Yzerman also signed 19 limited edition prints of himself painted by artist Murray Henderson to be auctioned off, with all funds destined to help defray Garrett's medical costs. "I'm pleased I was asked to get involved," Yzerman said. "I hope it helps raise even more money to help cover the costs of Tommy's treatments."

In Yzerman's mind, he doesn't figure he's done all that much, downplaying his contribution.

Anne-Marie Krappmann's become used to seeing Yzerman commit these sort of selfless acts time and again during her six years as the Red Wings' director of community relations.

What wasn't surprising to her was that Yzerman would be the most requested Red Wing when it came to charitable organizations. What she soon learned was that no one on the Red Wings was more accommodating to her requests.

"He's a big contributor of his time," Krappmann said. "We always get a lot of Make-A-Wish requests and the No. 1 guy the kids always want to meet is Steve Yzerman.

"Everything I've ever asked him to do, he's always been happy to do it. With children, I've seen him give so much. When we get an ill child who comes to meet with him, it's not like it's a handshake and a photo and that's it.

"I've seen him with those kids. He takes them around the rink, takes them into the room, makes sure they get to meet everyone on the team. He never leaves their side.

"He makes them feel like they're part of the team. And it's not like it's a one-time thing with him. He stays in touch. He calls to keep tabs on their progress."

Krappmann recalled a particular child from Denver. "Steve got the whole family tickets for one of our home playoff games last season and he paid for the whole trip.

"He didn't tell anyone else about this. He just did it because he wanted to do it."

When the Wings won the Stanley Cup in 2002, Yzerman, on crutches following knee surgery, dedicated one of his days with the Stanley Cup to three area hospitals - Children's Hospital of Michigan, William Beaumont Hospital and C.S. Mott Children's Hospital in Ann Arbor.

"There's a wing in Children's Hospital dedicated in his honor and I'll bet he doesn't even know about it," Krappmann said.

Some players launch foundations with lavish press conferences. That's simply not Yzerman's style. "During the course of my career, I played hockey and that was my No. 1 focus," Yzerman said. "Other guys set up foundations and put on golf tournaments. I just try to help out.

"I was more comfortable with letting everyone else do the work and I'll just show up when I'm needed and when I can. I prefer to play that kind of role."

As with all of his many special achievements, Yzerman would rather low-key it.

"Time permitting, I'm available to help out," he said.

To Stevie Y, charity is as simple as that.

"Away from the rink, I've had the opportunity to observe him and to bring charitable situations into this building, Make-A-Wish, particularly. And there was no one more giving of his time and again his energy for the less fortunate. He was tremendous.

"I had a lady that was dying of cancer here with her two daughters and her husband, and Steve was phenomenal, him and Darren McCarty. They weren't invited, they weren't asked. They saw this lady in a wheelchair and they came right over in the pre-game skate. She passed away a couple of months later, and in her husband's arms the night before she died, she said that the day at Joe Louis Arena was the most special day of her life."

— *Kerry Fraser*
NHL referee

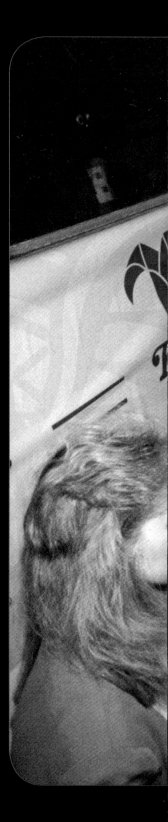

# The End of an Era

"Steve represents what leadership and commitment mean to the game of hockey. The loyalty he's shown his team and his community over his 22 seasons is unprecedented. He's one of the most respected guys in the league."

—Jason Smith
Edmonton Oilers captain

"Playing against Steve Yzerman was a great thrill; just to watch him on the ice and learn from him. Obviously, with the great rivalry we both were a part of those years, those were special moments as well. But more importantly, getting a chance to play together with the Canadian teams and All-Star games, getting a chance to know him and becoming friends, was something I'll always cherish. I got to learn firsthand what class was all about on and off the ice. Congratulations Steve, on an unbelievable career and all the memories you provided."

*—Joe Sakic*
Colorado Avalanche captain

"It was a tremendous honor to have had the opportunity to play not only with you but against you. You will always be known as one of the greatest players and leaders the NHL has ever seen. Best of luck to you and your family as you move on to the next stage of your career."

—Dallas Drake
St. Louis Blues captain

"Detroit is a great sport city and
we have great fans. I've been
treated so well by the fans not
only in Detroit but all around the
National Hockey League. I'm
very grateful for that."

– Steve Yzerman

"Steve was one of the most complete players to ever play the game. From offense, defense and a terrific face-off specialist. He was a tremendous leader and competitor with all of the intangibles and characteristics of a superstar."

—Scotty Bowman
NHL Hall of Fame
Head Coach

# Captains on The Captain

## Quotes from captains around the league on the career of number NINETEEN

"When I got to play with him in the Olympics, I was amazed for all of the things that he has accomplished, how down to earth he was. He made me feel comfortable and a part of it, which helps, and the way he respects other people really rubs off. He's had such an amazing career, one that you dream of. Congratulations and I'm sure he'll continue to be successful with whatever he does."

—Jarome Iginla
Calgary Flames captain

"Steve Yzerman is one of those players who makes you proud to be part of the National Hockey League. Even before I came to North America, I followed Steve's career. From his first day in the NHL until his retirement, he was a first-class player and person. He had an amazing career. When you consider all the legendary players with the Red Wings, Steve is right up there with them."

—Alexei Yashin
New York Islanders captain

"Steve was great fun to watch. He was a tremendous leader, and a great captain. He was a big influence on my decision to stay and sign a contract with New Jersey. It is rare to see a player of his skill level spend an entire career with one organization. That is special to me, and a lot of other players."

—Patrik Elias
New Jersey Devils captain

"When I look at Steve Yzerman, I think of highlight goals and great plays he made. But at the same time you got to look at his determination and his will to win. It allowed him to lead the team to three Stanley Cups. I think that's what made him what he was. '

—Daniel Alfredsson
Ottowa Senators captain

"He's a tremendous player, a classy player. He reminds me a lot of Ronnie Francis as far as their careers going on at the same time, being the same age, and having a similar presence on and off the ice. He carries himself with a lot of class and is very respected. He was a great player for the league and a great person for the league. When you can have guys like that as marquee players you're pretty lucky."

—Scott Mellanby
Atlanta Thrashers captain

"When you talk about all-time great leaders in the history of the National Hockey League, Steve Yzerman's name is clearly near the top of that list. As a fellow captain of an Original Six team, I understand the pride he had wearing the Red Wings sweater for 22 seasons, and admire the three Stanley Cup championships he brought to Detroit. He is a great example, both on and off the ice, for the next generation of NHL players."

—Jaromir Jagr
New York Rangers captain

"Steve Yzerman is a great example of how to be a leader. He had a great presence, not only in Detroit, but throughout the whole league. I have a lot of memories watching him play while growing up and I wish him all the best."

*—Patrick Marleau*
San Jose Sharks captain

"He's all class. I've had the chance to meet him a few times, practicing with him and playing golf. I haven't had the chance to be on any of his teams, so I can't really comment on his leadership, but he's just a consummate professional. He was and probably still is a great player, and he is all class."

*—Brendan Morrow*
Dallas Stars captain

"The thing that stands out the most for me was watching him in the 2002 playoffs. We played Detroit in the first round. We were up two games to none and he got them back in the series. He led the Red Wings to the Stanley Cup. Steve, basically, skated on one leg and that was so courageous and impressive, and it showed his leadership. I always looked up to him. He's such a classy person and I like how he carries himself. I have a lot of respect for him."

*—Markus Naslund*
Vancouver Canucks captain

"Steve Yzerman is certainly one of the best leaders of the game; an outstanding hockey player, he is known for his true commitment on and off the ice."

*—Saku Koivu*
Montreal Canadians captain

"We played against Steve and the Red Wings so many times when I was with Calgary in the Western Conference. What always struck me was how, on a team with so many all-stars and hall of fame players, he seemed to stand out. With his ability and the way he carried himself, he defined those Red Wing teams. He really was the ultimate captain in terms of his combination of skill and leadership."

*—Chris Clark*
Washington Capitals captain

"Steve was an exceptional ambassador for the game. His hard work and dedication both on and off the ice was recognized throughout the National Hockey League. His name will forever be linked to Detroit Red Wings hockey."

*—Olli Jokinen*
Florida Panthers captain

"He was probably the greatest leader of this sport. He was such a great player. His retirement is a big loss. Every time you lose a player like him it's a great loss for hockey."

*—Kimmo Timonen*
Nashville Predators captain

"He was a pretty quiet leader but whenever he said something, he would go out and prove it on the ice, producing results through his work ethic. The bigger the game, the better Stevie played. One of the things I've tried to do is lead by example. Before the season started, I had a chance to talk with him on what to expect and he helped run through a few of the little things for me. Hopefully I'll be around a long time to learn a lot from him."

—*Nicklas Lidstrom*
Detroit Red Wings captain

# NINETEEN
## QUICK FACTS

Yzerman won 2004 Michigan statewide poll to determine the most popular Detroit athlete of the past two decades. Barry Sanders, Al Kaline, Isiah Thomas and Gordie Howe followed him in the voting.

Brought To You By:

**Datapak Services Corporation**

*fulfilling the NEEDS of business*

www.datapakservices.com

# All-Star, World Champion and Olympian

# N I N E T E E N
## Q U I C K   F A C T S

Yzerman was the only rookie to appear in the 1984 NHL All-Star Game and at 18 years, 8 months and 22 days of age was the youngest player to perform in the league's All-Star Game.

*Thanks For The Memories.*

PACE
CUSTOM PRINTING

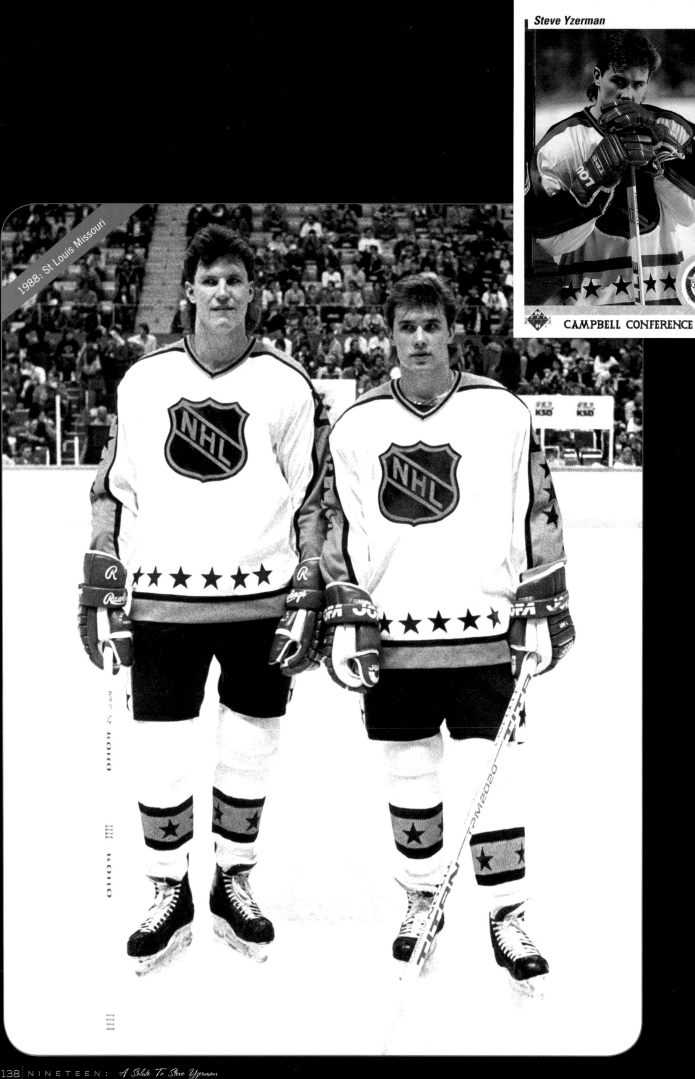

Steve Yzerman — Center

CAMPBELL CONFERENCE

1988: St Louis Missouri

1997: San Jose, Calif.

2000: Toronto, Ontario

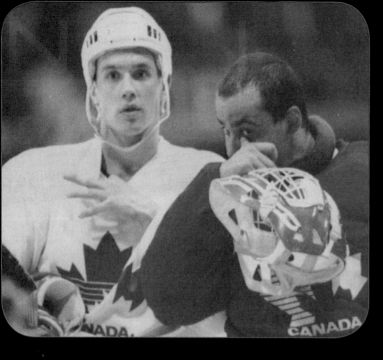

To the denizens of Hockeytown, he will always be the
captain. But there was another side to Steve Yzerman's career, one that unveiled his unique combination of character
and talent on the world stage.

"I like it, but it's a different game," Yzerman said of international hockey. "Bigger ice tends to slow things down,
really. It becomes more like soccer. It's harder to play de-
fence on the big ice. That's why everyone just backs up."

Yzerman wore the Canadian maple leaf on his chest before he ever wore the winged wheel. While still a Peterborough Pete, a year before he was drafted by Detroit, Yzerman joined the likes of Mario Lemieux, Dave Andreychuk,
Mike Vernon, Pat Verbeek and Sylvain Turgeon as part of
Canada's team at the 1983 World Junior Championships in
Leningrad, Russia, but that squad finished third behind the
Soviet Union and Czechoslovakia, proving once more the
lesson that Yzerman would harshly learn for years as a
member of the Red Wings - talent alone won't win a title.

After his rookie National Hockey League campaign,
Yzerman, just 19, was selected to the Canadian team for
the 1984 Canada Cup, but went pointless in four games as
Canada captured the trophy.

It was the first step in what would be a launching pad
for tremendous success in international hockey, but as with
his career in Detroit, there would be bumps in the road before Yzerman could achieve international hockey's ultimate
prize.

Canadian coach Mike Keenan stunningly cut Yzerman
from the 1987 and 1991 Canada Cup squads. "They did
what they thought was right," Yzerman said."It doesn't matter whether they were fair to me or not, whether I disagreed
or didn't disagree. That is the business and I had to live
with it."

What made the 1991 decision to drop Yzerman more
puzzling was that he'd been named the best forward of the
1990 world championships in Bern, Switzerland. Yzerman
won the scoring title with 20 points in 10 games, but in his
words, after Canada's fourth-place finish, "couldn't have
cared less" about the trophy he was presented. "We were
shooting for a gold medal and we didn't get it, so I was disappointed." Yzerman was part of Canadian teams at three
world tournaments, earning a silver medals in 1985 and
1989.

After his 1991 disappointment, he vowed never to give
up his summer to participate in a Team Canada training
camp for an international tournament, but relented and
joined the Canadian squad for the 1996 World Cup of
Hockey. "I thought about it for a long time whether I was
going to play or not," Yzerman recalled. "But a couple of
weeks after the season, I thought, 'I'm 31 years old and this
might be the last tournament like this I'll be around for.'"

Yzerman's troublesome right knee flared up during
training camp. After initial speculation that he'd need to be

eplaced, he was included on the final roster. "He was questionable, no doubt about it," Team Canada GM Glen Sather said. "He was a gamble, but he really wanted to play and he played great. I was happy for him." The end result was another disappointment, though. Canada fell to the U.S. in a three-game final.

He'd be proven wrong about one thing. Yzerman's greatest moment on the international stage was still to come. When the decision was made to include National Hockey League players at the 1998 Winter Olympics in Nagano, Japan, Yzerman was a natural choice to be part of the Canadian squad. Yzerman excelled in the tournament and used the experience as a springboard to help lead the Wings to another Stanley Cup. "I think when you're forced to elevate your game against the best players in the world, it can only be a positive," Yzerman said. "I know playing in Nagano served to boost my confidence and had a springboard effect as we headed into the playoffs."

The Olympic experience wasn't as rewarding. Canada lost in a semifinal shootout to the Czech Republic and dropped the bronze-medal game to Finland. "It went by very quickly," Yzerman remembered. "It was really exciting. One minute we're in a big game against the Czechs, next thing you know we're in overtime, 10 minutes later you're in a shootout and five minutes later you're done. It was a great experience but (the shootout) was excruciatingly disappointing."

Four years later, the NHLers would return to the Olympiad in Salt Lake City, but Yzerman, 36, figured his time had passed. Instead, he was among the initial eight players named to Canada's squad by executive director Wayne Gretzky. "When I played in Nagano, I thought that was going to be my one shot at an Olympic medal," Yzerman said. "When Wayne picked me to the team. I was surprised and really honored. I never expected to get another chance."

It was a chance that would be well taken. Canada was dumped 5-2 by Sweden in its opening game, but that's when Yzerman's unparalleled leadership skills came to the fore.

"The pace was too fast for us to rest out there, so we needed to pick it up," Canadian coach Pat Quinn explained. "And when we talked to the guys about doing it, it was (Joe) Sakic and Yzerman and (Mario) Lemieux who shortened their shifts and picked the pace up and that's why we became a competitive team. They were terrific leaders and that's what leadership is all about, your good guys showing the way for the rest of the team."

Yzerman also delivered on the ice. He scored the winner against Finland in the quarter-finals and registered a goal and an assist in Canada's semifinal victory over Belarus. "You've got to give a lot of credit to Steve Yzerman," Canadian assistant coach Jacques Martin said. "There's a guy who showed in the tournament a lot about what type of player he is. He came in hurt and played like there was no tomorrow. The guy was outstanding."

In the gold-medal game, Yzerman and Brendan Shanahan were triumphant over their Detroit teammates Chris Chelios and Brett Hull as Canada defeated the United States 5-2, giving the country its first golden moment in Olympic hockey since 1952. Yzerman and Shanahan joined former New York Islanders defenseman Ken Morrow (1980, USA) as the only players to win a Stanley Cup and an Olympic gold medal in the same season.

"I don't know what rapture means, but that was an awesome experience," Yzerman recalled. "Winning the gold medal is going to be remembered for a long time. It was a proud moment for every Canadian and I've got to imagine the whole country was watching."

Next to winning the gold medal, Yzerman's favorite memory is the fond recollection of how quickly that group of players united as one. "Access is pretty restrictive at the Olympics," Yzerman said. "After the game, we just sat in the room for about two hours - players, coaches and trainers - talking about what we'd just accomplished. It was something I'll never forget."

Gretzky virtually guaranteed Yzerman a spot on the 2006 Canadian Olympic team that would go to Torino, Italy, but a month into the 2005-06 NHL season, Yzerman recognized it was a position his performance level no longer warranted. He called Gretzky and asked to be removed from consideration for the team.

"I didn't feel I was playing well enough to hold one of the 13 (forward) spots," Yzerman said. "I'm very grateful for past opportunities representing my country, but there are too many good players playing too well for me to hold a spot on the roster."

In his final act on the international stage, Yzerman put the team ahead of himself and that is the true indication of leadership.

NINETEEN

"When I think of the Red Wings from my playing days I think of Steve Yzerman. He was a rare breed in that he played his entire career with one organization and was able in that time to lead his team from one of the bottom teams in the league to multiple Stanley Cups. He represented his team with great class and dignity and I am sure that he will continue to be a great contributor to the Red Wings franchise in whatever role that he chooses in the future. Congratulations on a great playing career and best wishes moving forward."

—*Mario Lemieux*
Hockey Great

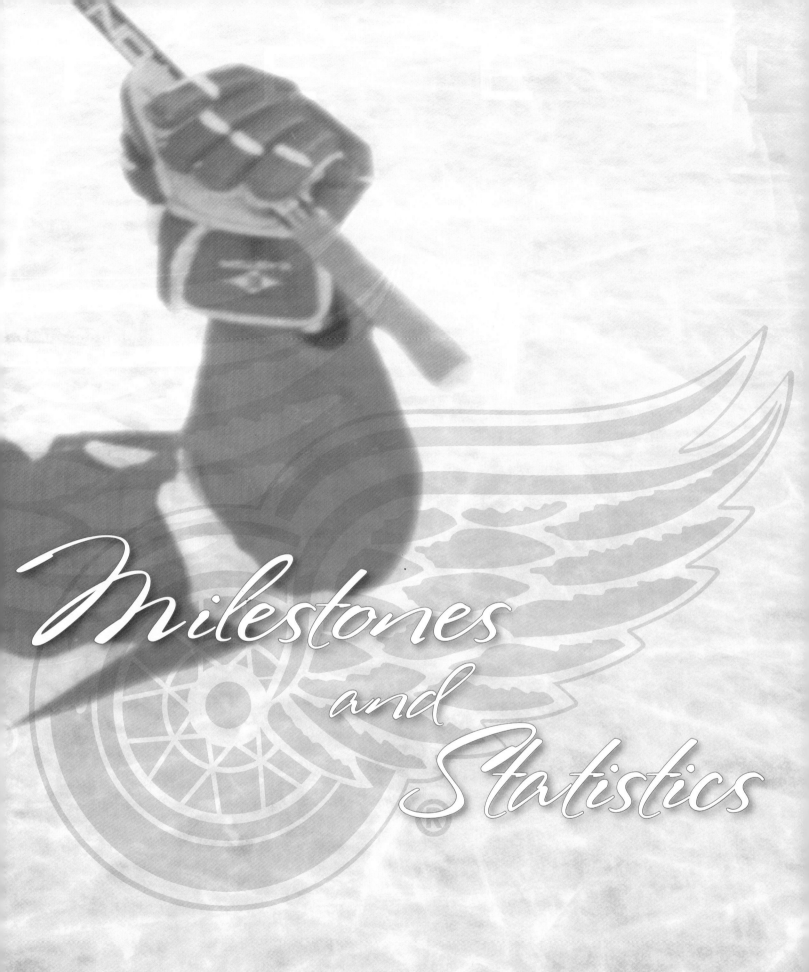

# Milestones and Statistics

# Milestone Goals

| No. | Date | Result | Assists |
| --- | --- | --- | --- |
| 1 | Oct. 5, 1983 | Detroit 6 at Winnipeg 6 | Ed Johnstone, Bob Manno |
| 100 | Jan. 17, 1986 | Quebec 2 at Detroit 3 | John Ogrodnick, Dave Barr |
| 200 | Dec. 30, 1988 | Detroit 3 at Hartford 4 | Gerard Gallant |
| 300 | Nov. 1, 1990 | Toronto 4 at Detroit 5 | Per Djoos |
| 400 | Nov. 13, 1992 | Pittsburgh 0 at Detroit 8 | Ray Sheppard, Bob Probert |
| 500 | Jan. 17, 1996 | Colorado 2 at Detroit 3 | Greg Johnson, Sergei Fedorov |
| 600 | Nov. 26, 1999 | Edmonton 2 at Detroit 4 | Steve Duchesne, Nicklas Lidstrom |

"I told him, 'Welcome aboard. And oh, by the way, I've got some stuff for you to sign. Five hundred goal-scorers' signatures are worth a lot of money.'"

*–Dino Ciccarelli*
Red Wings teammate and fellow 500-goal scorer
after Yzerman's 500th goal

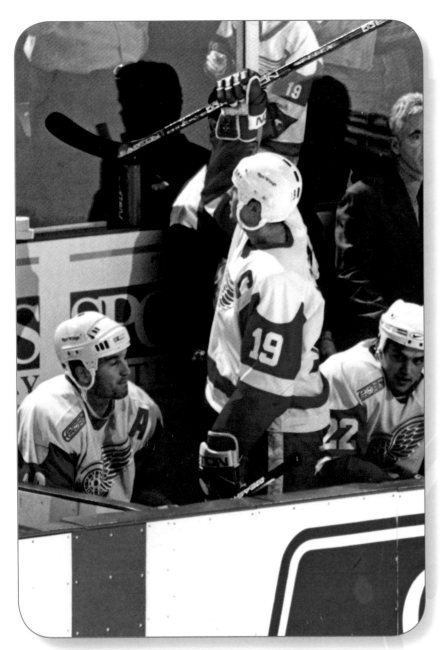

# Milestone Assists

| No. | Date | Result | Goal Scorer |
|---|---|---|---|
| 1 | Oct. 5, 1983 | Detroit 6 at Winnipeg 6 | Ed Johnstone |
| 100 | Mar. 2, 1985 | Detroit 2 at Minnesota 5 | Darryl Sittler |
| 200 | Nov. 7, 1987 | Detroit 3 at NY Islanders 4 | Petr Klima |
| 300 | Jan. 25, 1989 | Buffalo 6 at Detroit 3 | Joe Kocur |
| 400 | Mar. 27, 1990 | Buffalo 6 at Detroit 5 | Gerard Gallant |
| 500 | Feb. 11, 1992 | Detroit 3 at Toronto 4 | Keith Primeau |
| 600 | Oct. 13, 1992 | St. Louis 2 at Detroit 5 | Sergei Fedorov |
| 700 | Dec. 15, 1995 | New Jersey 1 at Detroit 3 | Bob Errey |
| 800 | Mar. 28, 1997 | Buffalo 1 at Detroit 2 | Larry Murphy |
| 900 | Nov. 17, 1999 | Detroit 7 at Vancouver 2 | Brendan Shanahan |
| 1,000 | Jan. 20, 2002 | Ottawa 2 at Detroit 3 | Mathieu Dandenault |
| 1,024* | Jan. 5, 2004 | Nashville 0 at Detroit 6 | Kris Draper |

*Surpassed Gordie Howe to become Detroit's all-time assists leader.

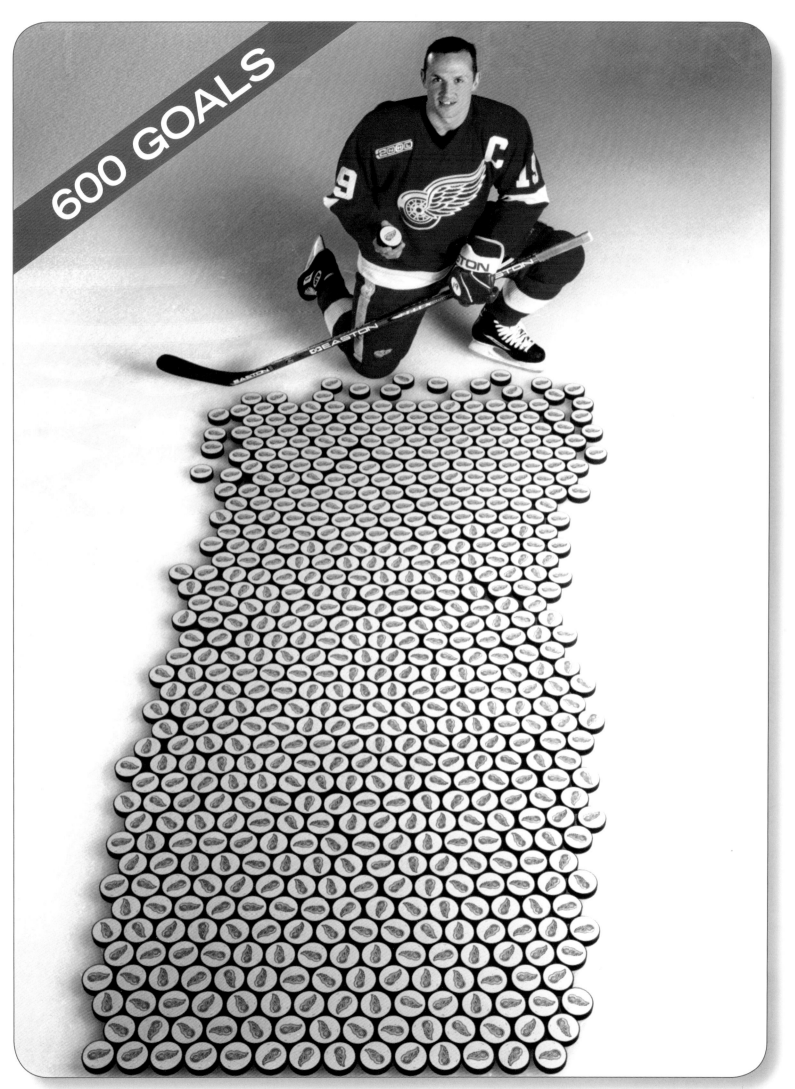

600 GOALS

| 800 | Mar. 31, 1991 | Detroit 1 at Chicago 5 | Goal |
| 900 | Apr. 14, 1992 | Detroit 7 at Minnesota 4 | Goal |
| 1,000 | Feb. 24, 1993 | Detroit 7 at Buffalo 10 | Assist |
| 1,100 | Mar. 4, 1994 | Toronto 6 at Detroit 5 | Goal |
| 1,200 | Dec. 29, 1995 | Detroit 2 at Dallas 1 | Assist |
| 1,300 | Jan. 5, 1997 | Detroit 5 at Chicago 5 | Goal |
| 1,400 | Mar. 29, 1998 | Buffalo 2 at Detroit 4 | Goal |
| 1,500 | Nov. 20, 1999 | Detroit 1 at Edmonton 2 | Assist |
| 1,600 | Feb. 23, 2001 | St. Louis 2 at Detroit 4 | Goal |
| 1,700 | Jan. 16, 2004 | Phoenix 3 at Detroit 3 | Assist |

# Hat Tricks

| Date | Opponent | Goaltender |
|------|----------|------------|
| Dec. 23, 1983 | Toronto | Mike Palmateer |
| Mar. 30, 1985 | Toronto | Ken Wregget |
| Jan. 3, 1988 | Winnipeg | Pokey Reddick |
| Feb. 6, 1988 | Montreal | Brian Hayward |
| Nov. 4, 1988 | Philadelphia | Mark Laforest |
| Nov. 12, 1988 | Philadelphia | Ron Hextall |
| Apr. 6, 1989* | Chicago | Alain Chevrier |
| Dec. 15, 1989 | Chicago | Jimmy Waite (1), Alain Chevrier (2) |
| Jan. 31, 1990 | Edmonton | Bill Ranford |
| Feb. 14, 1990 | Los Angeles | Ron Scott |
| Nov. 17, 1990 | Toronto | Jeff Reese |
| Dec. 22, 1990 | Winnipeg | Stephane Beauregard (2), Bob Essensa (1) |
| Jan. 26, 1991 | St. Louis | Vincent Riendeau |
| Apr. 4, 1991* | St. Louis | Vincent Riendeau (2), Pat Jablonski (1) |
| Dec. 3, 1991 | Calgary | Mike Vernon |
| Jan. 23, 1992 | Buffalo | Daren Puppa |
| Apr. 14, 1992 | Minnesota | Darcy Wakaluk (2), Empty Net (1) |
| Oct. 24, 1992 | St. Louis | Curtis Joseph (1), Guy Hebert (2) |
| Jan. 26, 1993 | Calgary | Mike Vernon |
| Feb. 14, 1993 | Chicago | Ed Belfour |
| May 8, 1996* | St. Louis | Jon Casey |
| Apr. 21, 1999* | Anaheim | Guy Hebert (2), Tom Askey (1) |

# Overtime Goals

## REGULAR SEASON

| Date | Opponent | Goaltender | Result |
|------|----------|------------|--------|
| Oct. 26, 1983 | Buffalo | Bob Sauve | Buffalo 5 at Detroit 6 |
| Oct. 18, 1988 | Chicago | Ed Belfour | Chicago 3 at Detroit 4 |
| Nov. 20, 1988 | Boston | Rejean Lemelin | Detroit 5 at Boston 4 |
| Nov. 2, 1995 | Boston | Blaine Lacher | Detroit 6 at Boston 5 |
| Jan. 31, 2001 | Columbus | Ron Tugnutt | Detroit 3 at Columbus 2 |
| Apr. 1, 2001 | Washington | Craig Billington | Washington 1 at Detroit 2 |
| Oct. 13, 2001 | NY Islanders | Chris Osgood | Detroit 5 at NY Islanders 4 |

## PLAYOFFS

| Date | Opponent | Goaltender | Result |
|------|----------|------------|--------|
| May 16, 1996 | St. Louis | Jon Casey | St. Louis 0 at Detroit 1 |

"I'm not big but I'm bigger than (Steve). I was going after someone else and I looked at Yzie and I pretty much gave him no choice but to drop the gloves. And after I told him 'at least he dropped his gloves.' "

—Chris Chelios
on his fight with Yzerman,
April 14, 1995, at
Chicago's United Center

## 50ᵗʰ *Goal in a Season*

| Date | Opponent | Goaltender |
|---|---|---|
| Mar. 1, 1988 | Buffalo | Tom Barrasso |
| Feb. 5, 1989 | Winnipeg | Pokey Reddick |
| Feb. 24, 1990 | NY Islanders | Glenn Healy |
| Mar. 30, 1991 | NY Rangers | Mike Richter |
| Mar. 10, 1993 | Edmonton | Bill Ranford |

## 60ᵗʰ *Goal in a Season*

| Date | Opponent | Goaltender |
|---|---|---|
| Mar. 1, 1989 | NY Islanders | Mark Fitzpatrick |

## 100ᵗʰ *Point in a Season*

| Date | Opponent | Goal/Assist |
|---|---|---|
| Feb. 27, 1988 | Quebec | Assist |
| Feb. 27, 1989 | Toronto | Goal |
| Feb. 18, 1990 | Montreal | Assist |
| Mar. 10, 1991 | St. Louis | Goal |
| Apr. 14, 1992 | Minnesota | Goal |
| Feb. 24, 1993 | Buffalo | Assist |

## 150ᵗʰ *Point in a Season*

| Date | Opponent | Goal/Assist |
|---|---|---|
| Mar. 24, 1989 | Toronto | Assist |

# 1,514 Games – 255 Teammates

| Player | Games | Player | Games | Player | Games | Player | Games |
|---|---|---|---|---|---|---|---|
| Nicklas Lidstrom | 908 | Dwight Foster | 141 | Mike Knuble | 54 | Bob Essensa | 13 |
| Sergei Fedorov | 746 | Darren Veitch | 137 | Torrie Robertson | 54 | Cory Cross | 12 |
| Shawn Burr | 633 | Bob Errey | 136 | Ed Johnstone | 52 | Bob McGill | 12 |
| Kris Draper | 583 | Bob Manno | 136 | Mikael Samuelsson | 51 | Dave Silk | 12 |
| Brendan Shanahan | 557 | Mathieu Schneider | 136 | Warren Young | 51 | Sean Avery | 11 |
| Yyacheslav Kozlov | 548 | Tim Taylor | 136 | Jamie Rivers | 50 | Wendel Clark | 11 |
| Gerard Gallant | 519 | Brent Gilchrist | 133 | Frank Cernik | 49 | Glenn Merkosky | 11 |
| Darren McCarty | 502 | Henrik Zetterberg | 132 | Yan Golubovsky | 48 | Steve Martinson | 10 |
| Martin Lapointe | 494 | Jamie Pushor | 131 | Borje Salming | 48 | Greg Millen | 10 |
| Joe Kocur | 491 | Manny Legace | 127 | Billy Carroll | 45 | Steve Richmond | 10 |
| Tomas Holmstrom | 474 | Colin Campbell | 125 | Maxim Kuznetsov | 45 | Jim Leavins | 9 |
| Kirk Maltby | 469 | Robert Lang | 125 | Dennis Vial | 44 | Brad Smith | 9 |
| Igor Larionov | 447 | Mike Sillinger | 119 | Doug Crossman | 43 | Jim Cummins | 8 |
| Steve Chiasson | 432 | Luc Robitaille | 115 | Eddie Mio | 43 | Dmitri Mironov | 8 |
| Bob Probert | 430 | Marc Habscheid | 111 | Steve Thomas | 43 | Anders Myrvold | 8 |
| Mathieu Dandenault | 422 | Gilbert Delorme | 109 | Micah Aivazoff | 42 | Bob Wilike | 8 |
| Vladimir Konstantinov | 421 | Mark Howe | 107 | Chris Cichocki | 41 | Troy Crowder | 7 |
| Doug Brown | 389 | Jim Nill | 106 | John Mokosak | 41 | Murray Eaves | 7 |
| Chris Osgood | 364 | Pat Verbeek | 104 | Joe Paterson | 41 | John Blum | 6 |
| Keith Primeau | 335 | Stacy Roest | 103 | Niklas Kronwall | 40 | Chris McRae | 6 |
| Rick Zombo | 324 | Dallas Drake | 102 | Basil McRae | 40 | Gary Shuchuk | 6 |
| Chris Chelios | 294 | Jason Woolley | 102 | Larry Trader | 40 | Tom Bissett | 5 |
| Larry Murphy | 280 | Jeff Sharples | 95 | Pierre Aubry | 39 | Mark Kumpel | 5 |
| Dave Barr | 277 | Brent Ashton | 94 | Jim Pavese | 39 | Nathan Robinson | 5 |
| Petr Klima | 262 | Mike Vernon | 93 | Curtis Joseph | 37 | Chris Tancill | 5 |
| Tim Cheveldae | 258 | Kevin Miller | 90 | Fredrik Olausson | 37 | Jesse Wallin | 5 |
| Mike O'Connell | 253 | Bobby Dollas | 89 | Darryl Laplante | 34 | Philippe Audet | 4 |
| Greg Stefan | 250 | Doug Halward | 88 | Barry Melrose | 34 | Allan Bester | 4 |
| John Ogrodnick | 248 | Joe Murphy | 88 | Brett Lebda | 33 | Bruce Eakin | 4 |
| Lee Norwood | 244 | Johan Garpenlov | 87 | Tomas Sandstrom | 33 | Chris Luongo | 4 |
| Ray Sheppard | 243 | Randy McKay | 82 | Doug Shedden | 33 | Steve Maltais | 4 |
| Aaron Ward | 240 | Harold Snepsts | 82 | Vincent Riendeau | 30 | Bill Ranford | 4 |
| Jimmy Carson | 239 | Mike Ramsey | 80 | Sam St. Laurent | 30 | Ray Staszak | 4 |
| Bob Rouse | 238 | Todd Gill | 78 | Kevin Hodson | 29 | Patrick Boileau | 3 |
| Randy Ladouceur | 236 | Adam Graves | 78 | Mike McEwen | 29 | Alain Chevrier | 3 |
| Yves Racine | 229 | Claude Loiselle | 78 | Greg C. Adams | 28 | Jody Gage | 3 |
| Dino Ciccarelli | 226 | Paul MacLean | 76 | Ken Wregget | 28 | Derian Hatcher | 3 |
| Jiri Fischer | 213 | Brad Marsh | 74 | Per Djoos | 26 | Ken Holland | 3 |
| Ron Duguay | 211 | Ric Seiling | 74 | Dale Krentz | 25 | Jimmy Howard | 3 |
| Adam Oates | 211 | Bernie Federko | 72 | Uwe Krupp | 25 | Peter Ing | 3 |
| John Chabot | 210 | Jamie Macoun | 71 | Rick MacLeish | 25 | Brian Johnson | 3 |
| Paul Ysebaert | 209 | Mark Mowers | 70 | Mark Laforest | 24 | Ulf Samuelsson | 3 |
| Reed Larson | 206 | Marc Bergevin | 69 | Tim Friday | 23 | Peter Dineen | 2 |
| Paul Coffey | 205 | Jason Williams | 69 | Miroslav Frycer | 23 | Mark Ferner | 2 |
| Boyd Devereaux | 202 | Rick Green | 65 | Bob Halkidis | 23 | David Gagnon | 2 |
| Brad McCrimmon | 202 | Stu Grimson | 65 | Gord Kruppke | 23 | Scott King | 2 |
| Greg Smith | 199 | Ray Whitney | 65 | Mark Lamb | 22 | Chris Kotsopoulos | 2 |
| John Barrett | 198 | Dave Lewis | 64 | Brian MacLellan | 22 | Marc Lamothe | 2 |
| Viacheslav Fetisov | 196 | Yuri Butsayev | 63 | Jim Hiller | 21 | Mark Major | 2 |
| Kelly Kisio | 193 | Kevin McClelland | 63 | Marc Rodgers | 21 | Andrew McKim | 2 |
| Pavel Datsyuk | 188 | Daniel Shank | 63 | Norm Maracle | 20 | Bill McDougall | 2 |
| Glen Hanlon | 177 | Terry Carkner | 62 | Robert Picard | 20 | Mark Pederson | 2 |
| Danny Gare | 173 | Andreas Lilja | 61 | Mike Krushelnyski | 19 | Ryan Barnes | 1 |
| Doug Houda | 169 | Darryl Sittler | 61 | Ted Nolan | 19 | Sergei Bautin | 1 |
| Lane Lambert | 169 | Mel Bridgman | 60 | Andre St. Laurent | 19 | Jeff Brubaker | 1 |
| Tim Higgins | 166 | Kris King | 58 | Jason York | 19 | Valtteri Filppula | 1 |
| Sheldon Kennedy | 164 | Blake Dunlop | 57 | Steve Konroyd | 18 | Miroslav Ihnacak | 1 |
| Brent Fedyk | 161 | Johan Franzen | 57 | Darryl Bootland | 16 | Tomas Kopecky | 1 |
| Steve Duchesne | 156 | Alan Kerr | 57 | Murray Craven | 15 | Don MacLean | 1 |
| Greg Johnson | 152 | Corrado Micalef | 57 | Dmitri Bykov | 14 | Dean Morton | 1 |
| Ivan Boldirev | 150 | Paul Woods | 57 | Milan Chalupa | 14 | Kyle Quincey | 1 |
| Brad Park | 147 | Daniel Cleary | 56 | Jiri Hudler | 14 | Wes Walz | 1 |
| Anders Eriksson | 142 | Dave (Tiger) Williams | 55 | Tony McKegney | 14 | B.J. Young | 1 |
| Brett Hull | 142 | Dominik Hasek | 54 | Marc Potvin | 14 | | |

# 196 Playoff Games – 161 Playoff Teammates

| Player | Games | Player | Games | Player | Games | Player | Games |
|---|---|---|---|---|---|---|---|
| Nicklas Lidstrom | 154 | Adam Oates | 25 | Alan Kerr | 9 | Blake Dunlop | 4 |
| Sergei Fedorov | 145 | Dominik Hasek | 23 | Manny Legace | 9 | Johan Franzen | 4 |
| Kris Draper | 132 | Boyd Devereaux | 24 | Jim Nill | 9 | Niklas Kronwall | 4 |
| Darren McCarty | 132 | Brent Gilchrist | 24 | Ulf Samuelsson | 9 | Lane Lambert | 4 |
| Kirk Maltby | 109 | Jamie Macoun | 23 | Mark Kumpel | 8 | Brett Lebda | 4 |
| Brendan Shanahan | 101 | Rick Zombo | 23 | Bob McGill | 8 | Andreas Lilja | 4 |
| Igor Larionov | 98 | Dave Barr | 22 | John Ogrodnick | 8 | Brad Marsh | 4 |
| Tomas Holmstrom | 84 | Tim Taylor | 22 | Pat Verbeek | 8 | Bill Ranford | 4 |
| Vyacheslav Kozlov | 75 | Anders Eriksson | 21 | John Barrett | 7 | Mikael Samuelsson | 4 |
| Martin Lapointe | 75 | Fredrik Olausson | 21 | Dallas Drake | 7 | Pierre Aubry | 3 |
| Viacheslav Fetisov | 74 | Greg Stefan | 21 | Ron Duguay | 7 | Rick Green | 3 |
| Vladimir Konstantinov | 71 | Tomas Sandstrom | 20 | Brent Fedyk | 7 | Mike Knuble | 3 |
| Doug Brown | 65 | Brent Ashton | 19 | Sheldon Kennedy | 7 | Claude Loiselle | 3 |
| Bob Rouse | 64 | Mel Bridgman | 19 | Kelly Kisio | 7 | Corrado Micalef | 3 |
| Shawn Burr | 60 | Petr Klima | 19 | Randy Ladouceur | 7 | Joe Murphy | 3 |
| Joe Kocur | 59 | Mathieu Schneider | 19 | Reed Larson | 7 | Joe Paterson | 3 |
| Chris Chelios | 57 | Paul Ysebaert | 19 | Bob Manno | 7 | Gary Shuchuk | 3 |
| Chris Osgood | 55 | Henrik Zetterberg | 19 | Randy McKay | 7 | Brad Smith | 3 |
| Keith Primeau | 53 | Jimmy Carson | 18 | Dmitri Mironov | 7 | Larry Trader | 3 |
| Mathieu Dandenault | 46 | Brad McCrimmon | 18 | Marc Potvin | 7 | Jim Hiller | 2 |
| Gerard Gallant | 45 | Marc Bergevin | 16 | Ric Seiling | 7 | Ed Johnstone | 2 |
| Bob Probert | 43 | Tim Higgins | 16 | Greg Smith | 7 | Kris King | 2 |
| Paul Coffey | 39 | Kevin Miller | 16 | Jason Woolley | 7 | Uwe Krupp | 2 |
| Pavel Datsyuk | 39 | Robert Lang | 15 | Ivan Boldirev | 6 | Norm Maracle | 2 |
| Larry Murphy | 39 | Jason Williams | 15 | Doug Crossman | 6 | Vincent Riendeau | 2 |
| Mike Vernon | 39 | Greg Johnson | 14 | Dwight Foster | 6 | Stacy Roest | 2 |
| Brett Hull | 38 | Dave Lewis | 14 | Danny Gare | 6 | Darryl Sittler | 2 |
| Dino Ciccarelli | 36 | Harold Snepsts | 14 | Johan Garpenlov | 6 | Allan Bester | 1 |
| Jiri Fischer | 34 | Darren Veitch | 14 | Doug Houda | 6 | Troy Crowder | 1 |
| Steve Duchesne | 32 | Glen Hanlon | 12 | Mike Krushelnyski | 6 | Kevin Hodson | 1 |
| Ray Sheppard | 32 | Curtis Joseph | 12 | Brad Park | 6 | Steve Konroyd | 1 |
| Steve Chiasson | 30 | Todd Gill | 11 | Torrie Robertson | 6 | Dale Krentz | 1 |
| Aaron Ward | 30 | Stu Grimson | 11 | Jeff Sharples | 6 | Rick MacLeish | 1 |
| Bob Errey | 28 | Derian Hatcher | 11 | Adam Graves | 5 | Bill McDougall | 1 |
| Luc Robitaille | 27 | Mark Lamb | 11 | Marc Habscheid | 5 | Eddie Mio | 1 |
| Mike Ramsey | 26 | Mike Sillinger | 11 | Paul MacLean | 5 | Mark Mowers | 1 |
| Yves Racine | 25 | Ray Whitney | 11 | Jamie Pushor | 5 | Jamie Rivers | 1 |
| Tim Cheveldae | 25 | Wendel Clark | 10 | Steve Thomas | 5 | Jrir Slegr | 1 |
| Gilbert Delorme | 25 | John Chabot | 9 | Dmitri Bykov | 4 | | |
| Lee Norwood | 25 | Bobby Dollas | 9 | Colin Campbell | 4 | | |
| Mike O'Connell | 25 | Mark Howe | 9 | Daniel Cleary | 4 | | |

# 692 Goals – 1,107 Assists from Teammates

| Player | Assists | Player | Assists | Player | Assists | Player | Assists |
|---|---|---|---|---|---|---|---|
| Gerard Gallant | 84 | Doug Halward | 9 | Brett Hull | 3 | Bob Essensa | 1 |
| Nicklas Lidstrom | 76 | Vyacheslav Kozlov | 9 | Jim Pavese | 3 | Miroslav Frycer | 1 |
| Sergei Fedorov | 52 | Rick Zombo | 9 | Luc Robitaille | 3 | Johan Garpenlov | 1 |
| John Ogrodnick | 39 | John Chabot | 8 | Stacy Roest | 3 | Bob Halkidis | 1 |
| Steve Chiasson | 35 | Steve Duchesne | 7 | Bob Rouse | 3 | Derian Hatcher | 1 |
| Brendan Shanahan | 34 | Doug Houda | 7 | Borje Salming | 3 | Ed Johnstone | 1 |
| Bob Probert | 29 | Mark Howe | 7 | Daniel Shank | 3 | Alan Kerr | 1 |
| Shawn Burr | 27 | Brad McCrimmon | 7 | Brent Ashton | 2 | Kelly Kisio | 1 |
| Dino Ciccarelli | 27 | Randy Ladouceur | 6 | Doug Brown | 2 | Steve Konroyd | 1 |
| Ron Duguay | 27 | Robert Lang | 6 | Daniel Cleary | 2 | Dale Krentz | 1 |
| Lee Norwood | 26 | Mathieu Schneider | 6 | Tim Cheveldae | 2 | Niklas Kronwall | 1 |
| Yves Racine | 24 | Jeff Sharples | 6 | Pavel Datsyuk | 2 | Uwe Krupp | 1 |
| Ray Sheppard | 24 | Greg Smith | 6 | Boyd Devereaux | 2 | Mike Krushelnyski | 1 |
| Igor Larionov | 22 | Pat Verbeek | 6 | Anders Eriksson | 2 | Andreas Lilja | 1 |
| Darren McCarty | 22 | Jimmy Carson | 5 | Jiri Fischer | 2 | Chris Luongo | 1 |
| Dave Barr | 21 | Kris Draper | 5 | Brent Gilchrist | 2 | Jamie Macoun | 1 |
| Larry Murphy | 20 | Viacheslav Fetisov | 5 | Marc Habscheid | 2 | Bob Manno | 1 |
| Paul Ysebaert | 20 | Kirk Maltby | 5 | Glen Hanlon | 2 | Corrado Micalef | 1 |
| Paul Coffey | 19 | Adam Oates | 5 | Dave Lewis | 2 | Ed Mio | 1 |
| Tomas Holmstrom | 17 | Jason Williams | 5 | Brad Marsh | 2 | Anders Myrvold | 1 |
| Reed Larson | 17 | John Barrett | 4 | Mike McEwen | 2 | Fredrik Olausson | 1 |
| Vladimir Konstantinov | 16 | Danny Gare | 4 | Randy McKay | 2 | Chris Osgood | 1 |
| Paul MacLean | 16 | Rick Green | 4 | Jim Nill | 2 | Jamie Pushor | 1 |
| Brad Park | 16 | Greg Johnson | 4 | Robert Picard | 2 | Ulf Samuelsson | 1 |
| Darren Veitch | 16 | Sheldon Kennedy | 4 | Tomas Sandstrom | 2 | Darryl Sittler | 1 |
| Petr Klima | 15 | Lane Lambert | 4 | Doug Shedden | 2 | Dennis Vial | 1 |
| Ivan Boldirev | 13 | Joe Murphy | 4 | Mike Sillinger | 2 | Aaron Ward | 1 |
| Joe Kocur | 11 | Ray Whitney | 4 | Harold Snepsts | 2 | Jason Woolley | 1 |
| Martin Lapointe | 11 | Mel Bridgman | 3 | Tim Taylor | 2 | Ken Wregget | 1 |
| Keith Primeau | 11 | Chris Cichocki | 3 | Henrik Zetterberg | 2 | Warren Young | 1 |
| Chris Chelios | 10 | Mathieu Dandenault | 3 | Terry Carkner | 1 | Jason York | 1 |
| Bernie Federko | 10 | Gilbert Delorme | 3 | Frank Cernik | 1 | | |
| Mike O'Connell | 10 | Per Djoos | 3 | Doug Crossman | 1 | | |
| Bob Errey | 9 | Brent Fedyk | 3 | Dallas Drake | 1 | | |

# 70 Playoff Goals – 114 Playoff Assists from Teammates

| Player | Assists | Player | Assists | Player | Assists | Player | Assists |
|---|---|---|---|---|---|---|---|
| Nicklas Lidstrom | 14 | Ivan Boldirev | 2 | Rick Zombo | 2 | Joe Kocur | 1 |
| Brendan Shanahan | 9 | Chris Chelios | 2 | Dave Barr | 1 | Vladimir Konstantinov | 1 |
| Sergei Fedorov | 8 | Dino Ciccarelli | 2 | John Barrett | 1 | Robert Lang | 1 |
| Bob Errey | 5 | Mathieu Dandenault | 2 | Shawn Burr | 1 | Reed Larson | 1 |
| Tomas Holmstrom | 5 | Steve Duchesne | 2 | Wendel Clark | 1 | Paul MacLean | 1 |
| Paul Coffey | 4 | Ron Duguay | 2 | Doug Crossman | 1 | Kirk Maltby | 1 |
| Darren McCarty | 4 | Vyacheslav Kozlov | 2 | Kris Draper | 1 | Larry Murphy | 1 |
| Bob Probert | 4 | Martin Lapointe | 2 | Brent Gilchrist | 1 | Brad Park | 1 |
| Steve Chiasson | 3 | Igor Larionov | 2 | Doug Houda | 1 | Ulf Samuelsson | 1 |
| Viacheslav Fetisov | 3 | Lee Norwood | 2 | Mark Howe | 1 | Greg Stefan | 1 |
| Gerard Gallant | 3 | Adam Oates | 2 | Brett Hull | 1 | Ray Whitney | 1 |
| Ray Sheppard | 3 | Mike O'Connell | 2 | Petr Klima | 1 | Paul Ysebaert | 1 |

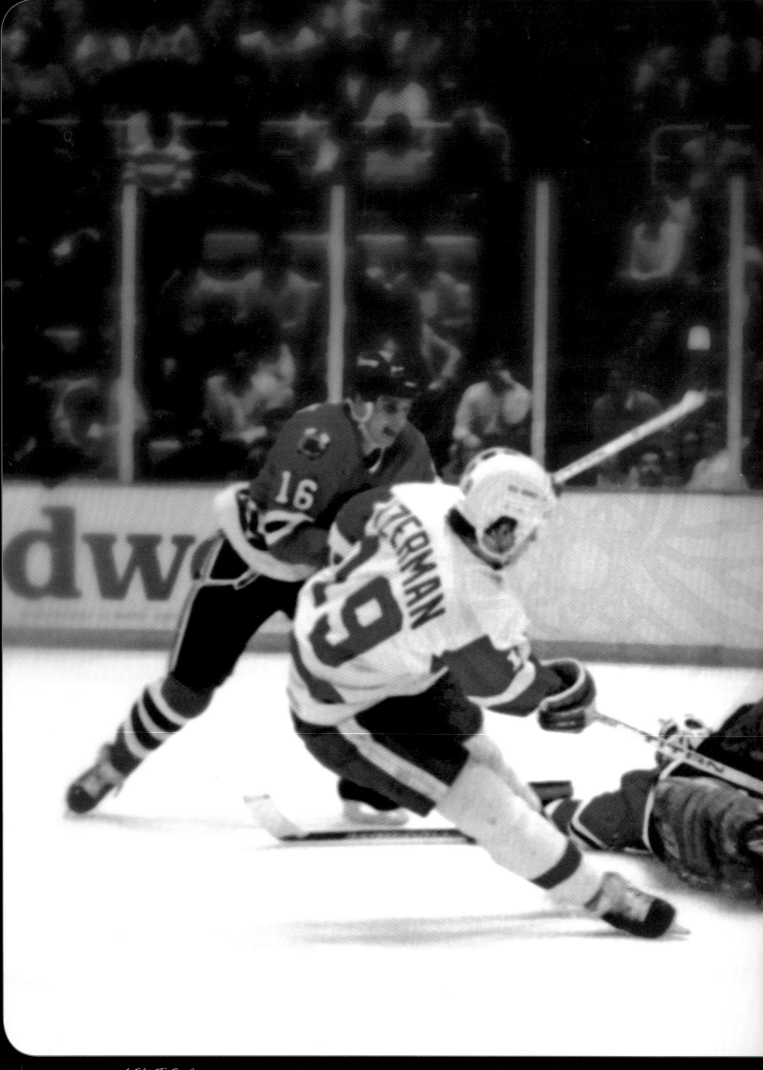

# 692 Goals against 150 Goaltenders

| Goaltender | Goals Against | Goaltender | Goals Against | Goaltender | Goals Against | Goaltender | Goals Against |
|---|---|---|---|---|---|---|---|
| Ed Belfour | 21 | Mark Laforest | 6 | Darren Pang | 3 | Scott Clemmensen | 1 |
| Bill Ranford | 21 | Jeff Reese | 6 | Ron Scott | 3 | Ty Conklin | 1 |
| Grant Fuhr | 16 | Daniel Berthiaume | 5 | Billy Smith | 3 | Jim Craig | 1 |
| Kirk McLean | 16 | Allan Bester | 5 | Tommy Soderstrom | 3 | Byron Dafoe | 1 |
| Andy Moog | 14 | Jeff Hackett | 5 | Doug Soetaert | 3 | Marc Denis | 1 |
| Mike Vernon | 14 | Dominik Hasek | 5 | Robb Stauber | 3 | Tom Draper | 1 |
| Greg Millen | 13 | Glenn Healy | 5 | Rick Tabaracci | 3 | Darren Eliot | 1 |
| Patrick Roy | 13 | Pat Jablonski | 5 | Kevin Weekes | 3 | Robert Esche | 1 |
| Guy Hebert | 12 | Rejean Lemelin | 5 | Wendell Young | 3 | Scott Fankhouser | 1 |
| Kelly Hrudey | 12 | Bob Mason | 5 | Stephane Beauregard | 2 | Joaquin Gage | 1 |
| Daren Puppa | 12 | Pokey Reddick | 5 | Tim Bernhardt | 2 | Martin Gerber | 1 |
| John Vanbiesbrouck | 12 | Dwayne Roloson | 5 | Craig Billington | 2 | Jean-Sebastien Giguere | 1 |
| Tom Barrasso | 11 | Marty Turco | 5 | John Blue | 2 | Rick Heinz | 1 |
| Don Beaupre | 11 | Murray Bannerman | 4 | Tim Cheveldae | 2 | Denis Herron | 1 |
| Jon Casey | 11 | Fred Brathwaite | 4 | Wade Flaherty | 2 | Kevin Hodson | 1 |
| Bob Essensa | 11 | Frank Caprice | 4 | Bob Froese | 2 | Bruce Hoffort | 1 |
| Felix Potvin | 11 | Mike Dunham | 4 | John Garrett | 2 | Arturs Irbe | 1 |
| Ken Wregget | 11 | Manny Fernandez | 4 | Al Jensen | 2 | Darren Jensen | 1 |
| Brian Hayward | 10 | Mario Gosselin | 4 | Olaf Kolzig | 2 | Brent Johnson | 1 |
| Curtis Joseph | 10 | Patrick Lalime | 4 | Jason LaBarbera | 2 | Trevor Kidd | 1 |
| Vincent Riendeau | 10 | Gilles Meloche | 4 | Pelle Lindbergh | 2 | Miikka Kiprusoff | 1 |
| Kari Takko | 9 | Evgeni Nabokov | 4 | Roland Melanson | 2 | Rick Knickle | 1 |
| Chris Terreri | 9 | Chris Osgood | 4 | Damian Rhodes | 2 | Blaine Lacher | 1 |
| Alain Chevrier | 8 | Steve Passmore | 4 | Dominic Roussel | 2 | Gary Laskoski | 1 |
| Mike Liut | 8 | Tommy Salo | 4 | Peter Sidorkiewicz | 2 | Pascal Leclaire | 1 |
| Clint Malarchuk | 8 | Mikhail Shtalenkov | 4 | Jamie Storr | 2 | Norm Maracle | 1 |
| Bob Sauve | 8 | Garth Snow | 4 | Vesa Toskala | 2 | Jussi Markkanen | 1 |
| Rick Wamsley | 8 | Jocelyn Thibault | 4 | Roman Turek | 2 | Markus Mattsson | 1 |
| Stephane Fiset | 7 | Tomas Vokoun | 4 | Jimmy Waite | 2 | Tyler Moss | 1 |
| Mark Fitzpatrick | 7 | Darcy Wakaluk | 4 | Steve Weeks | 2 | Rich Parent | 1 |
| Ron Hextall | 7 | Kay Whitmore | 4 | David Aebischer | 1 | Steve Penney | 1 |
| Peter Ing | 7 | Richard Brodeur | 3 | Craig Anderson | 1 | Glenn Resch | 1 |
| Mike Palmateer | 7 | Sean Burke | 3 | Zac Bierk | 1 | Pat Riggin | 1 |
| Pete Peeters | 7 | Dan Cloutier | 3 | Dan Bouchard | 1 | Corey Schwab | 1 |
| Mike Richter | 7 | Jacques Cloutier | 3 | Brian Boucher | 1 | Steve Shields | 1 |
| Ron Tugnutt | 7 | Don Edwards | 3 | Mario Brunetta | 1 | Warren Skorodenski | 1 |
| J.C. Bergeron | 6 | Corey Hirsch | 3 | Jim Carey | 1 | Empty Net | 21 |
| Nikolai Khabibulin | 6 | Doug Keans | 3 | Roman Cechmanek | 1 | | |

# 70 Playoff Goals against 28 Goaltenders

| Goaltender | Goals Against | Goaltender | Goals Against | Goaltender | Goals Against | Goaltender | Goals Against |
|---|---|---|---|---|---|---|---|
| Goalie | Goals | Dan Cloutier | 3 | Vincent Riendeau | 2 | Warrren Skorodenski | 1 |
| Jon Casey | 8 | Mike Liut | 3 | Bob Sauve | 2 | Garth Snow | 1 |
| Grant Fuhr | 6 | Ron Hextall | 2 | Tom Askey | 1 | Tomas Vokoun | 1 |
| Patrick Roy | 6 | Arturs Irbe | 2 | Murray Bannerman | 1 | Jimmy Waite | 1 |
| Alain Chevrier | 5 | Brent Johnson | 2 | Martin Brodeur | 1 | Ken Wregget | 1 |
| Guy Hebert | 5 | Nikolai Khabibulin | 2 | Pat Jablonski | 1 | | |
| Felix Potvin | 4 | Miikka Kiprusoff | 2 | Jamie McLennan | 1 | | |
| Ed Belfour | 3 | Olaf Kolzig | 2 | Andy Moog | 1 | | |

# 1063 Regular Season Assists

| Player | Goals | Player | Goals | Player | Goals | Player | Goals |
|---|---|---|---|---|---|---|---|
| Gerard Gallant | 97 | Martin Lapointe | 10 | Sheldon Kennedy | 3 | Wendel Clark | 1 |
| Brendan Shanahan | 73 | Lee Norwood | 10 | Greg Johnson | 3 | Doug Crossman | 1 |
| Sergei Fedorov | 65 | Brett Hull | 9 | Lane Lambert | 3 | Bernie Federko | 1 |
| John Ogrodnick | 46 | Igor Larionov | 9 | Robert Lang | 3 | Viacheslav Fetisov | 1 |
| Nicklas Lidstrom | 43 | Kirk Maltby | 9 | Adam Oates | 3 | Johan Franzen | 1 |
| Ray Sheppard | 43 | Yves Racine | 9 | Darryl Sittler | 3 | Miroslav Frycer | 1 |
| Dino Ciccarelli | 41 | Darren Veitch | 8 | Rick Zombo | 3 | Todd Gill | 1 |
| Bob Probert | 35 | Kevin Miller | 7 | Chris Chelios | 2 | Rick Green | 1 |
| Steve Chiasson | 32 | Jason Williams | 7 | Chris Cichocki | 2 | Tim Higgins | 1 |
| Darren McCarty | 28 | Tomas Sandstrom | 6 | Brent Gilchrist | 2 | Mark Howe | 1 |
| Paul MacLean | 26 | Brent Ashton | 5 | Adam Graves | 2 | Mike Knuble | 1 |
| Ron Duguay | 25 | Brent Fedyk | 5 | Marc Habscheid | 2 | Uwe Krupp | 1 |
| Keith Primeau | 22 | Danny Gare | 5 | Doug Halward | 2 | Maxim Kuznetsov | 1 |
| Dave Barr | 21 | Johan Garpenlov | 5 | Doug Houda | 2 | Randy Ladouceur | 1 |
| Vyacheslav Kozlov | 21 | Larry Murphy | 5 | Ed Johnstone | 2 | Rick MacLeish | 1 |
| Ivan Boldirev | 19 | Mike O'Connell | 5 | Kelly Kisio | 2 | Kevin McClelland | 1 |
| Tomas Holmstrom | 17 | Jeff Sharples | 5 | Brad Marsh | 2 | Brad McCrimmon | 1 |
| Pat Verbeek | 16 | Tim Taylor | 5 | Jim Nill | 2 | Randy McKay | 1 |
| Paul Ysebaert | 16 | Anders Eriksson | 4 | Jamie Pushor | 2 | Dmitri Mironov | 1 |
| Shawn Burr | 15 | Brad Park | 4 | Bob Rouse | 2 | Dean Morton | 1 |
| Joe Kocur | 15 | Luc Robitaille | 4 | Borje Salming | 2 | Joe Murphy | 1 |
| Bob Errey | 13 | Mathieu Schneider | 4 | Mike Sillinger | 2 | Ric Seiling | 1 |
| Petr Klima | 13 | Doug Shedden | 4 | Greg Smith | 2 | Brad Smith | 1 |
| Reed Larson | 13 | Warren Young | 4 | Aaron Ward | 2 | Harold Snepsts | 1 |
| Jimmy Carson | 11 | Doug Brown | 3 | Ray Whitney | 2 | Jason York | 1 |
| Paul Coffey | 10 | John Chabot | 3 | John Barrett | 1 | Paul Woods | 1 |
| Mathieu Dandenault | 10 | Gilbert Delorme | 3 | Mel Bridgman | 1 | Jason Woolley | 1 |
| Kris Draper | 10 | Boyd Devereaux | 3 | Dmitri Bykov | 1 | Chris Tancill | 1 |
| Vladimir Konstantinov | 10 | Bobby Dollas | 3 | Colin Campbell | 1 | Henrik Zetterberg | 1 |
| | | Steve Duchesne | 3 | Frank Cernik | 1 | | |

# 115 Playoff Assists

| Player | Goals | Player | Goals | Player | Goals | Player | Goals |
|---|---|---|---|---|---|---|---|
| Nicklas Lidstrom | 13 | Martin Lapointe | 3 | Luc Robitaille | 2 | Lee Norwood | 1 |
| Brendan Shanahan | 11 | Brent Ashton | 2 | Mel Bridgman | 1 | Mike O'Connell | 1 |
| Sergei Fedorov | 9 | Dave Barr | 2 | Chris Chelios | 1 | Yves Racine | 1 |
| Gerard Gallant | 8 | Doug Brown | 2 | Mark Howe | 1 | Torrie Robertson | 1 |
| Dino Ciccarelli | 7 | Ron Duguay | 2 | Greg Johnson | 1 | Mathieu Schneider | 1 |
| Tomas Holmstrom | 6 | Brent Gilchrist | 2 | Kelly Kisio | 1 | Greg Smith | 1 |
| Darren McCarty | 4 | Brett Hull | 2 | Petr Klima | 1 | Ray Whitney | 1 |
| Bob Probert | 4 | Robert Lang | 2 | Joe Kocur | 1 | Jason Williams | 1 |
| Ray Sheppard | 4 | Igor Larionov | 2 | Kirk Maltby | 1 | | |
| Paul Coffey | 3 | Fredrik Olausson | 2 | Kevin Miller | 1 | | |
| Vyacheslav Kozlov | 3 | Keith Primeau | 2 | Larry Murphy | 1 | | |

# Career Scoring Statistics by Rink

| Arena (Team) | GP | G | A | PTS | Arena (Team) | GP | G | A | PTS |
|---|---|---|---|---|---|---|---|---|---|
| Joe Louis Arena (Detroit) | 765 | 331 | 566 | 897 | HP Pavilion (San Jose) | 20 | 4 | 9 | 13 |
| Maple Leaf Gardens (Toronto) | 51 | 29 | 45 | 74 | Xcel Energy Center (Minnesota) | 8 | 4 | 7 | 11 |
| St. Louis Arena (St. Louis) | 39 | 23 | 25 | 48 | America West Arena (Phoenix) | 11 | 1 | 9 | 10 |
| Met Center (Minnesota) | 37 | 17 | 31 | 48 | Corel Center (Ottawa) | 6 | 5 | 4 | 9 |
| Chicago Stadium (Chicago) | 39 | 18 | 29 | 47 | Thunderdome (Tampa Bay) | 4 | 3 | 4 | 7 |
| Rexall Place (Edmonton) | 34 | 24 | 22 | 46 | TD Banknorth Garden (Boston) | 7 | 2 | 5 | 7 |
| The Forum (Los Angeles) | 26 | 16 | 24 | 40 | Staples Center (Los Angeles) | 9 | 2 | 5 | 7 |
| Pengrowth Saddledome (Calgary) | 36 | 16 | 14 | 30 | Miami Arena (Florida) | 3 | 1 | 5 | 6 |
| Winnipeg Arena (Winnipeg) | 19 | 16 | 13 | 29 | HSBC Arena (Buffalo) | 4 | 1 | 5 | 6 |
| United Center (Chicago) | 27 | 10 | 18 | 28 | Cow Palace (San Jose) | 4 | 3 | 2 | 5 |
| Pacific Coliseum (Vancouver) | 17 | 12 | 15 | 27 | Pepsi Center (Colorado) | 8 | 2 | 3 | 5 |
| Boston Garden (Boston) | 15 | 11 | 14 | 25 | McNichols Sports Arena (Colorado) | 7 | 1 | 4 | 5 |
| Nassau Coliseum (NY Islanders) | 19 | 10 | 15 | 25 | RBC Center (Carolina) | 4 | 4 | 0 | 4 |
| The Spectrum (Philadelphia) | 15 | 12 | 12 | 24 | St. Pete Times Forum (Tampa Bay) | 4 | 2 | 2 | 4 |
| Memorial Auditorium (Buffalo) | 15 | 9 | 13 | 22 | Wachovia Center (Philadelphia) | 4 | 2 | 2 | 4 |
| Madison Square Garden (NY Rangers) | 19 | 10 | 12 | 22 | Nationwide Arena (Columbus) | 9 | 1 | 3 | 4 |
| GM Place (Vancouver) | 18 | 8 | 12 | 20 | Philips Arena (Atlanta) | 1 | 1 | 2 | 3 |
| Reunion Arena (Dallas) | 17 | 7 | 13 | 20 | Bell Centre (Montreal) | 6 | 1 | 2 | 3 |
| Mellon Arena (Pittsburgh) | 20 | 5 | 14 | 19 | American Airlines Center (Dallas) | 5 | 2 | 0 | 2 |
| Capital Centre (Washington) | 15 | 9 | 9 | 18 | BankAtlantic Center (Florida) | 2 | 1 | 1 | 2 |
| Arrowhead Pond (Anaheim) | 20 | 8 | 10 | 18 | Richfield Coliseum (Cleveland) | 1 | 1 | 0 | 1 |
| Continental Airlines Arena (New Jersey) | 20 | 6 | 11 | 17 | Glendale Arena (Phoenix) | 6 | 1 | 0 | 1 |
| Colisee de Quebec (Quebec) | 14 | 10 | 6 | 16 | Bradley Center (Milwaukee) | 1 | 0 | 1 | 1 |
| Hartford Civic Center (Hartford) | 15 | 4 | 12 | 16 | MCI Center (Washington) | 2 | 0 | 1 | 1 |
| Montreal Forum (Montreal) | 15 | 8 | 7 | 15 | Air Canada Center (Toronto) | 3 | 0 | 1 | 1 |
| Expo Hall (Tampa Bay) | 4 | 6 | 9 | 15 | Ottawa Civic Centre (Ottawa) | 2 | 0 | 0 | 0 |
| Savvis Center (St. Louis) | 25 | 7 | 7 | 14 | Greensboro Coliseum (Carolina) | 3 | 0 | 0 | 0 |
| Gaylord Entertainment Center (Nashville) | 14 | 5 | 8 | 13 | | | | | |

**CAREER TOTALS  Games: 1514     Goals: 692     Assists: 1063     Points: 1755**

# Playoff Rinks

| Arena (City) | GP | G | A | PTS | Arena (City) | GP | G | A | PTS |
|---|---|---|---|---|---|---|---|---|---|
| Joe Louis Arena (Detroit) | 101 | 40 | 64 | 104 | Wachovia Center (Philadelphia) | 2 | 2 | 0 | 2 |
| Savvis Center (St. Louis) | 11 | 6 | 7 | 13 | Gaylord Entertainment Center (Nashville) | 3 | 1 | 1 | 2 |
| Rexall Place (Edmonton) | 6 | 3 | 6 | 9 | Met Center (Minnesota) | 3 | 0 | 2 | 2 |
| Chicago Stadium (Chicago) | 9 | 3 | 6 | 9 | Pepsi Center (Colorado) | 6 | 0 | 2 | 2 |
| St. Louis Arena (St. Louis) | 6 | 4 | 3 | 7 | Continental Airlines Arena (New Jersey) | 2 | 1 | 0 | 1 |
| Maple Leaf Gardens (Toronto) | 6 | 1 | 6 | 7 | Staples Center (Los Angeles) | 2 | 0 | 1 | 1 |
| McNichols Sports Arena (Colorado) | 9 | 3 | 3 | 6 | MCI Center (Washington) | 2 | 0 | 1 | 1 |
| GM Place (Vancouver) | 3 | 2 | 3 | 5 | Reunion Arena (Dallas) | 5 | 0 | 1 | 1 |
| America West Arena (Phoenix) | 3 | 1 | 3 | 4 | United Center (Chicago) | 1 | 0 | 0 | 0 |
| Winnipeg Arena (Winnipeg) | 3 | 2 | 1 | 3 | RBC Center (Carolina) | 2 | 0 | 0 | 0 |
| Arrowhead Pond (Anaheim) | 6 | 1 | 2 | 3 | Pengrowth Saddledome (Calgary) | 2 | 0 | 0 | 0 |
| San Jose Arena (San Jose) | 3 | 0 | 3 | 3 | | | | | |

# Most Seasons With One Professional Team

| Player | Sport | Team | Seasons |
|---|---|---|---|
| Alex Delvecchio | NHL | Detroit Red Wings | 1950 to 1974 |
| Brooks Robinson | MLB | Baltimore Orioles | 1955 to 1977 |
| Carl Yastrzemski | MLB | Boston Red Sox | 1961 to 1983 |
| *Steve Yzerman* | *NHL* | *Detroit Red Wings* | *1983 to 2006* |
| Stan Mikita | NHL | Chicago Blackhawks | 1958 to 1980 |
| Al Kaline | MLB | Detroit Tigers | 1953 to 1974 |
| Mel Ott | MLB | New York Giants | 1926 to 1947 |
| Stan Musial | MLB | St. Louis Cardinals | 1941 to 1963 |
| Walter Johnson | MLB | Washington Senators | 1907 to 1927 |
| Cal Ripken Jr. | MLB | Baltimore Orioles | 1981 to 2001 |
| Jean Beliveau | NHL | Montreal Canadiens | 1950 to 1971 |
| Henri Richard | NHL | Montreal Canadiens | 1955 to 1975 |
| Red Faber | MLB | Chicago White Sox | 1914 to 1933 |
| Darrell Green | NFL | Washington Redskins | 1983 to 2002 |
| Jackie Slater | NFL | Los Angeles/St. Louis Rams | 1976 to 1995 |
| John Havlicek | NBA | Boston Celtics | 1963 to 1978 |

# N I N E T E E N
## Q U I C K   F A C T S

Yzerman became the second player in Red Wings history to tally 600 NHL goals, beating Edmonton's Tommy Salo Nov. 11, 1999 at Joe Louis Arena. Gordie Howe was the first Red Wing reach 600 goals, beating Montreal's Gump Worsley Nov. 27, 1965.

*The Lauzon Family*
*&*
*The Cotton Family*          *Congratualate Number Nineteen*

DETROIT RED WINGS
LEGENDS

# ONE

*Number Retired on March 6, 1994*

## TERRY SAWCHUCK

# SEVEN

*Number Retired on November 10, 1991*

## TED LINDSAY

# NINE

*Number Retired on March 12, 1972*

## GORDIE HOWE

# T E N

*Number Retired on November 10, 1991*

# ALEX DELVECCHIO

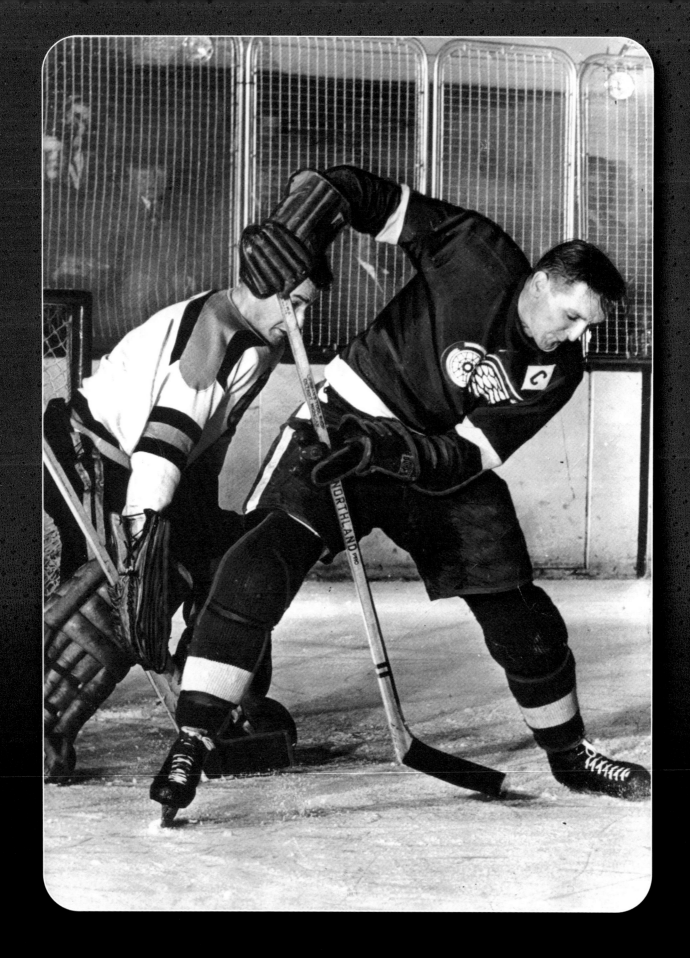

# T W E L V E
*Number Retired on April 22, 1995*

## SID ABEL

# NINETEEN

*Number Retired on January 2, 2007*

## STEVE YZERMAN

*Welcome Home Dad!*